MAXIM GUN AND SMALL ARMS.

$$\frac{40}{\text{W.O.}}$$
1533

NOMENCLATURE OF PARTS, STRIPPING, ASSEMBLING, ACTION, JAMS, MISSFIRES, FAILURES, AND INSPECTION OF:

(1.) Rifles, Short, **M.L.E.**
(2.)   ,,   Charger Loading **M.L.E.**
(3.) Pistols, Webley.
(4.) **Maxim** ·303-inch.

COMPILED IN THE FIELD ARTILLERY AND SMALL ARMS BRANCH, ORDNANCE COLLEGE. (REVISED EDITION—1911.)

The Naval & Military Press Ltd

Published by

The Naval & Military Press Ltd

Unit 5 Riverside, Brambleside
Bellbrook Industrial Estate
Uckfield, East Sussex
TN22 1QQ England

Tel: +44 (0)1825 749494

www.naval-military-press.com
www.nmarchive.com

ROYAL
ARMOURIES

The Library & Archives Department at the
Royal Armouries Museum, Leeds, specialises
in the history and development of armour
and weapons from earliest times to the
present day. Material relating to the
development of artillery and modern
fortifications is held at the Royal
Armouries Museum, Fort Nelson.

For further information contact:
Royal Armouries Museum, Library, Armouries Drive, Leeds, West Yorkshire LS10 1LT

Or visit the Museum's website at
www.armouries.org.uk

MAGAZINE RIFLES IN THE SERVICE.

Long Rifles.

Magazine Lee-Metford (M.L.M.) Mark I Issued 1889.

,,	,,	,,	,,	,,	I*	,,	1892.
,,	,,	,,	:,	,,	II	,,	1894.
,,	,,	,,	,,	,,	II*	,,	1895.
,,	,, Enfield	(M.L.E.)	,,	I	,,		1896.
,,	,,	,,	,,	,,	I*	,,	1899.

These rifles will be found chiefly in the Colonial Forces. The Metford system of rifling gave excessive wear of the barrel when cordite was used as the propellant, so the Enfield system with fewer and deeper grooves was introduced. As the Metford barrels wear out, they are replaced by Enfield barrels.

A large number of M.L.M., Mark II* and M.L.E. rifles have been converted to charger-loading, and with an improved back-sight are known as M.L.E. charger-loading rifles and are for issue to the Territorial Force. Many of the later patterns of Long Rifles have been converted to Short Rifles, known as converted Mark II, II*, and IV.

Rifle, Charger-Loading, Magazine Lee-Enfield, Mark I*.

= Converted from M.L.M., Mark II*, and M.L.E., Mark I and I*, for the use of the Territorial Force. First issued in 1908.

Short Rifles.

Rifle, short, Magazine Lee-Enfield, Mark I, issued 1904.

| ,, | ,, | ,, | ,, | ,, | ,, | I* | ,, | 1907. |
| ,, | ,, | ,, | ,, | ,, | ,, | III | ,, | 1907. |

In addition to the above, the later patterns of the Long Rifle have been converted to Short Rifles, as follows:—

R.S.M.L.E. converted Mark II, conforming to S.R. Mark I.

| ,, | ,, | ,, II* | ,, | ,, | ,, I*. |
| ,, | ,, | ,, IV | ,, | ,, | ,, III. |

The converted rifles conform to the new rifles of the same date, except for a few components taken from the old rifle and utilised in the conversion instead of manufacturing new components to the pattern adopted in Short Rifles.

The "Short Rifle" was introduced in 1904 to replace the "Long Rifle" and the "Carbine." It is issued to all branches of the Service, and the following are the chief points of difference between it and the Long Rifle :—

1. Average Marks I, I*, II and II* about 1 lb. lighter, Marks III and IV about 8 ozs. lighter.

2. Barrel smaller in diameter and 5 inches shorter.

3. Improved sighting arrangements.

4. Adapted for charger loading.

5. Trigger has a double pull-off.

6. Barrel completely covered by handguards and stock. Great attention is paid to the correct adjustment of the stock-fore-end and of the nose-cap. The barrel is connected to the stock by the inner band and spring, with ·002″ clearance between barrel and band. The opening in the nose-cap for the barrel is elliptical, with a spring stud to press the barrel against the top of the opening. Clearance ·002″. The function of the spring stud is to retain the barrel in an unvarying position with reference to the nose-cap.

Directions for Stripping Rifles, Short, Magazine Lee-Enfield Marks I, I* and III. Also Converted Short Rifles Marks II, II* and IV, and C.L. Rifles.

Tools.—None but the authorised tools should be used, and then only for the purpose for which intended, *e.g.*, a small screwdriver should not be used to remove or replace large screws, nor should a large screw driver be used for small screws, &c. The tools should be laid out on the bench to the right of the vice, close to the flower, and the component parts of the rifle, as stripped, on the left side of vice. This arrangement prevents the tools and parts of rifle from becoming mixed.

The following is a list of the tools which are supplied for use when stripping and assembling rifles.

Designation of Tool.	No.	Use of Tool.
Anvil, stock butt, M.L.E.R.S. (Short rifles).	1	For attaching stock butts that have slightly swelled.
Anvil, stock butt, M.R., (R.C.L.).	1	
Braces, Armourers	1	For use with the various bits.
Bits, Screwdriver:— Butt plate screw	1	For removing or replacing screws butt plate...
Stock bolt	1	For removing, replacing, or tightening stock bolt.
Clams, Armourers, standing vice.	1	Cork or buff lined for use with the vice when gripping the rifle to prevent damage to the woodwork, &c.
Drifts, fore-end M.L.M.R. Mark II.	1	For removal and replacement of the stock fore-end.
Drifts, pin, fixing, washer, pin axis sight back.	1	For removing and replacing the pin fixing. *Note.*—No other drift should be used or damage will be caused to the washer.
Drifts, sight axis pin ...	1	For removing axis pins.

Designation of Tool.	No.	Use of Tool.
Drifts, wire, large and small	1	For removing any screws which stick after being unscrewed.
Drivers, Screw :—		
Armourers { large	1	For screws band inner, nose cap back, guard trigger front, dial sight fixing screw. It is also used for removing and replacing the sear spring.
small	1	For screws band outer, swivels piling and butt, nose cap front, disc marking butt, ejector, guard trigger back, sear, spring sight back, stop charger guide, and screw spring sight aperture.
Extractor Axis, M.L.M. ...	1	For screws bed back sight, cut off, extractor, keeper fine adjustment, and screw nut keeper striker (early marks).
Fork Dial Sight	1	For screw sight dial pivot, and (with Mk. III and IV Rifles) screw catch slide back.
Implement, Action, M.L.E. R. Short.	1	Various uses.
Implement, Action, M.L.M.	1	Pattern "D" for M.L.E. charger loading rifles.
Hammers, rivetting, 4 oz. ...	1	Various uses.
Pincers, Armourers	1	Do.
Pliers, flat-nose	1	Do.
Testers, trigger pull, Mk. II.	1	For weighing various springs.
Tools, Extractor Spring ...	1	For removing and replacing extractor spring.
Tools removing handguard No. 1	1	For removal of rear handguards of rifles, short, Mk. III. and converted Mk. IV.
No. 2	1	For removal of handguards of charger loading M.L.E. rifles.
Tools removing striker R.S.M.L.E.	1	When striker is struck so that it cannot be removed by the bolt head.
Tools removing striker, Pattern B.	1	For use with M.L.E.C.L. rifles.

Designation of Tool.	No.	Use of Tool.
Tools removing wad stock bolt	1	For withdrawing the wad stock bolt from the butt.
Tools removing plate keeper screw wind-gauge.	1	For lifting the keeper plate from its recess.
Vices, standing, 36 lb. ...	1	For holding the rifle while stripping.
Gauges, distance of bolt from end of chamber. ⎰ ·064″	1	For testing minimum distance allowed between face of bolt-head and end of chamber.
⎱ ·074″	1	For testing maximum distance allowed between face of bolt-head and end of chamber.
Gauges, Armourers. Pistol Webley :— Hammer projection and radius of point.	1	⎱ For use with Webley pistols.
Distance of cylinder from face of body, ·052-inch rejecting.	1	⎰
Gauges, projection of stock bolt through body.	1	To gauge and ensure that the stock bolt is properly screwed home, and that the projection is not excessive.
Gauge striker point (for height and figure).	1	Protrusion from ·04″—·042″.
Pilot pins (not a service store) coned-point, thus—	1	Should be made as required for assisting in the replacement of axis pins for back sights, &c.

The following gauge plugs are used to test the wear of barrels for exchange.

Gauge armourers, plug ·303 inch, ·307 inch, ·308 inch, 310 inch, and plug lead No. 2.

Plug ·309 inch and plug lead No. 1 are for use with the maxim gun.

The following tools are supplied for cleaning barrels and clearing obstructions in the bore such as broken pull-throughs, rust, broken cases in chamber, &c. :—

Designation of Tool.	No.	Use of Tool.
Rods, cleaning, ·303 in. :—		
Nos. 1	1	For Jute, suitable for rifle and carbine.
,, 2	1	For use with brass wire, rifle. Can be used for M.L.E. rifles, short, only when fitted with Bush, stop, rod, No. 2.
,, 3	1	For use with brass wire, carbine.
,, 4	1	For use with brass wire, rifle, short M.L.E.
Bush, stop, rod cleaning, ·303, No. 2.	1	For use with rod No. 2 when used with short rifles.
Muzzle guides :—		
No. 2	1	Carbine, cavalry, ·303 in. and rifle, short, M.L.E. For use when using the above rods to prevent "bell-mouthing" of muzzle.
No. 1	1	Rifle and carbine artillery, ·303 in. For use when using the above rods to prevent "bell-mouthing" of muzzle.
Plugs, clearing, split, M.L.M. rifle.	1	For removal of split case and bullet envelope from chamber or bore of magazine arms.
Plugs, plain, ·303 in. arms ...	1	Tapped at end to fit on rod No. 2, for use in removal of bullet envelope, and in tamping when removing a broken pull-through, &c.
Tools, clearing, ·303 in. arms :—		
Bits, screw	1	For removal of broken pull-through, &c.
,, spoon	1	
Bush, bit, screw	1	
Rod, No. 2	1	Screwed at end to take above clearing bits and plugs.
Rods, cleaning, cylinder, pistol, Webley.	1	For use with brass wire.

SHORT RIFLE, MAGAZINE LEE-ENFIELD (MARK III)

Plate I.

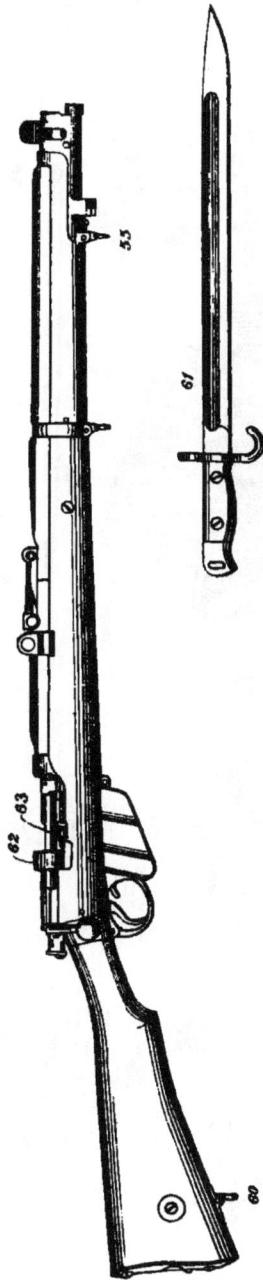

46J. I4257/3i2. 2000. 8. II.

Malby & Sons. Lith.

SHORT RIFLE, MAGAZINE LEE-ENFIELD (MARK III).

Plate II.

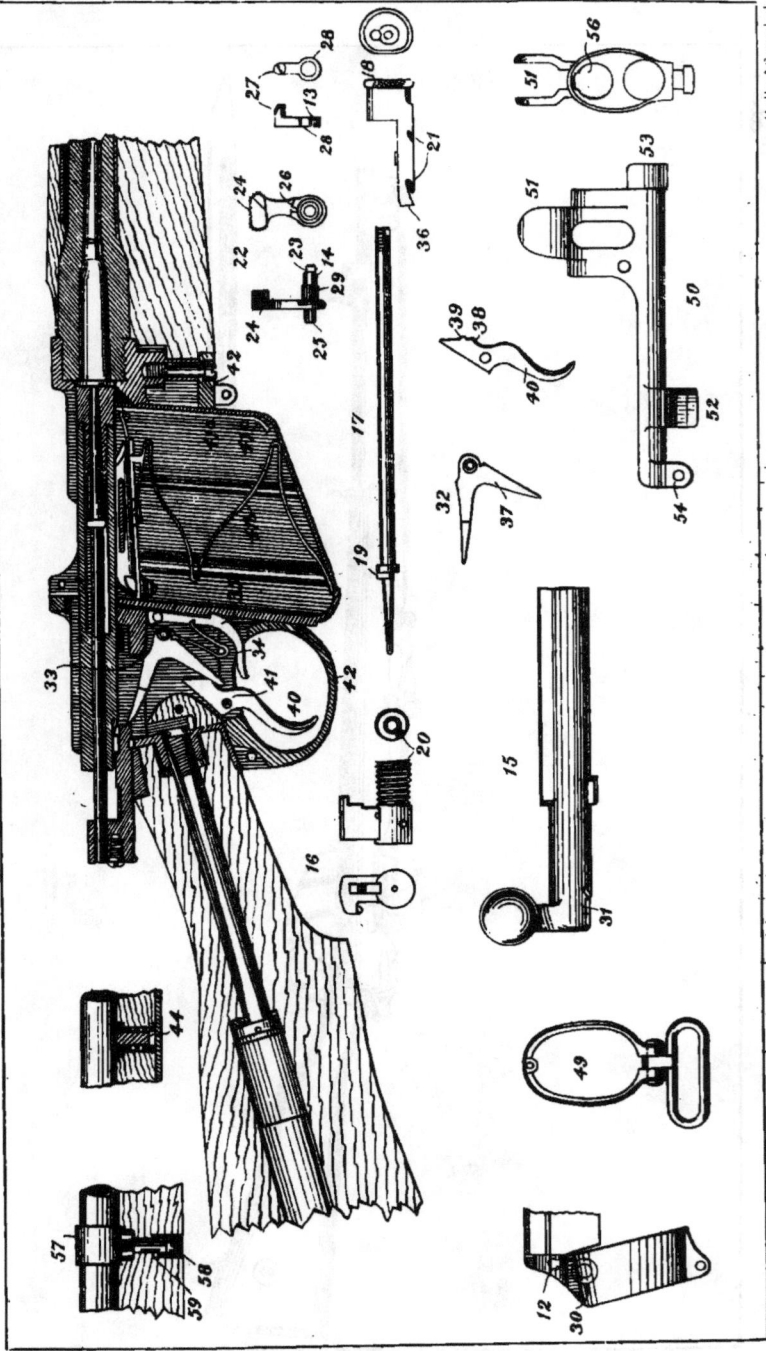

Malby & Sons, Lith.

463. 14257/3/2. 2000 8.11.

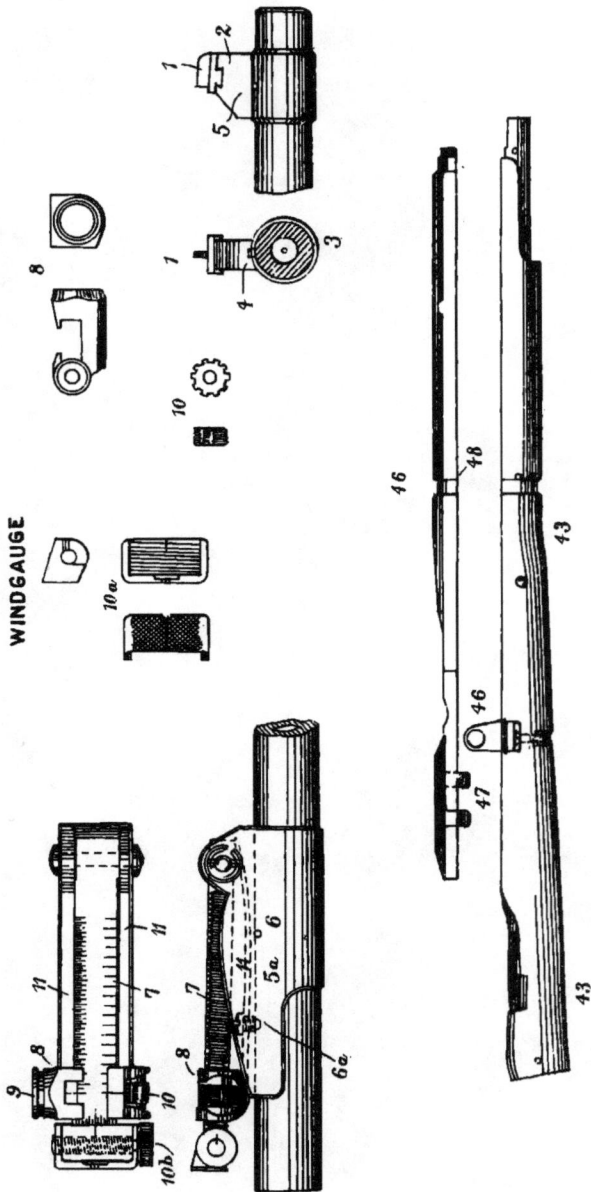

SHORT RIFLE, MAGAZINE LEE-ENFIELD (MARK III)

Plate III.

WINDGAUGE

463. 14257/3l2. 2000. 8. II.

PLATE IV.

NAMES OF THE PARTS OF RIFLE, SHORT M.L.E., MARK III, REFERRED TO IN PLATES I. TO III.

1.	Blade foresight	31.	Bolt cam grooves
2.	Foresight block	32.	Sear
3.	Band foresight block	33.	„ seating
4.	Key „ „	34.	„ spring
5.	Crosspin „ „	35.	Magazine catch
5A.	Backsight bed	36.	Full bent of cocking piece
6.	„ „ crosspin	37.	Short arm of sear
6A.	„ „ sight spring screw	38.	⎱ Trigger ribs
7.	Backsight leaf	39.	⎰
8.	„ slide	40.	Trigger
9.	„ slide catch	41.	Trigger axis pin
10.	„ fine adjustment worm wheel	41A.	Magazine case
10A.	Windgauge	41B.	„ platform spring
10B.	„ screw	41C.	„ auxiliary „
11.	Backsight ramps	42.	Guard trigger
12.	Seating for safety catch	43.	Stock fore-end
13.	Safety catch	44.	Spring and stud fore-end
14.	Locking bolt stem	45.	Protector backsight
15.	Bolt	46.	Handguard front and rear
16.	„ head	47.	Spring handguard gear
17.	Striker	48.	Lower band groove
18.	Cocking piece	49.	Lower band
19.	Striker collar with stud	50.	Nosecap
20.	Bolt head tenon	51.	Protector foresight
21.	Cocking piece locking recesses	52.	Sword bar
22.	Locking bolt	53.	Boss for ring of sword bayonet crosspiece
23.	„ „ flat	54.	Swivel seating
24.	„ „ thumbpiece	55.	„ piling
25.	„ „ aperture sight stem	56.	Nosecap barrel opening
26.	„ „ stop pin recesses	57.	Inner band
27.	„ „ safety catch stem	58.	„ „ screw
28.	„ „ safety catch arm	59.	„ „ „ spring
29.	„ „ screw threads	60.	Butt sling swivel
30.	„ „ seating	61.	Sword bayonet, pattern 07
		62.	Bridge charger guide
		63.	Cut-off

STRIPPING. R.S.M.L.E. (All marks.)

Position of the Rifle when clamped in the Vice.—The rifle is fixed in the vice in five different positions both for stripping and assembling. (See Figs. **1, 2, 3, 5,** and 6.) In each position a certain number of the components are removed or replaced, as the case may be; it is most important that the rifle should be correctly placed in the vice, as otherwise it is liable to become damaged.

1st Position. Fig. 1.

Clamped in the vice at the band outer, magazine uppermost, muzzle pointing towards the right and butt end resting on the left horse, as shown in Fig. 1.

In this position strip the following parts and lay them out on the bench to the left of the vice:—

Screws nose-cap, front and rear; outer band; and swivel.

(*Note.*—The swivel screw may be difficult to remove on account of its end being splayed with a centre punch, the screw-driver should be kept pressed hard into the slot of the screw while turning to prevent distortion.)

The rifle is now shifted to the 2nd position.

2ND POSITION.   FIG. 2.

Note.—The horse should be carried a little further to the right than shown, so that the barrel rests on it either in front or immediately in rear of the backsight.

Clamped at the parallel portion of the stock butt, magazine up and muzzle to the right (see Fig. 2).

Remove the following :—The nose cap, tapping it off gently towards the front with a mallet or hammer, with drift fore-end applied to the sword bar.

Next remove the outer band, raise the backsight and remove the handguards front, and rear (with the Mark III and converted Mark IV rifles, the handguard rear must be removed with the tool removing handguard, No. 1, before fixing the rifle in the vice.) Unscrew and remove inner band screw with its spiral spring; remove magazine; screw guard, front and rear, and guard; raise aperture sight, and with the wooden drift and hammer remove the fore-end, take out the stud and spring from the front of fore-end.

To strip the fore-end.—If necessary the fore-end can now be stripped as follows :—

Dial Sight.—Fix the stock fore-end in the vice with the dial towards you, with driver, screw, fork, dial sight, remove screw dial sight pivot, spring, and dial sight pointer. Next turn the fore-end so that its right side is towards you and with the large screwdriver remove the screw fixing dial sight; the dial sight plate can now be lifted out of its recess in the fore-end.

(*Note.*—Never attempt to remove the dial plate before removing the large fixing screw which passes through the stock fore-end from right to left.)

The small pin on the inner face of the dial plate is intended to prevent any turning movement of the plate; care should, therefore, be taken to prevent damage to the pin or its recess in the fore-end. With the Marks III and Converted IV rifles, the protector backsight can be removed by unscrewing the nut and screw; it may be necessary to hold the nut or screw with a second screwdriver should both nut and screw turn without coming apart.

The rifle can now be shifted to the third position.

3RD POSITION. FIG. 3.

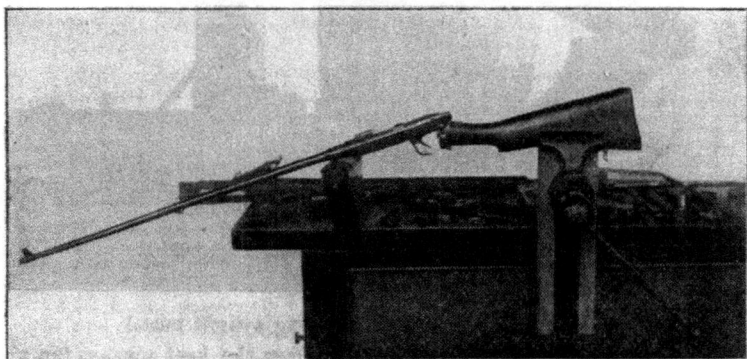

Clamped in the vice at the parallel portion of the stock butt, backsight uppermost, muzzle to the left and resting on the left horse. (*See* Fig. 3.)

In this position remove the following parts :—
Butt plate screws (using the brace and bit supplied), butt plate with trap and spring; wad stock bolt, then with the brace and bit with metal collar, unscrew the stock bolt until it is quite clear of the body, which is indicated by the jumping of the screwed end against the body as the bolt is turned.

Note.—Never attempt to remove this bolt without first removing the fore-end. While unscrewing the bolt the left hand should hold the body so as to prevent the barrel and body falling to the ground if loose on the stock butt.

Now remove the "stock butt." To do this if the butt is tight in the body proceed as follows :—
Remove the rifle from the vice and grasp it with the left hand round the barrel in rear of the backsight, and with the right hand at the small of the butt, the toe of the latter up and backsight down. (*See* Fig. 4.)

Fig. 4.

(Showing the method of removing a tight butt.)

Now strike the butt about 3 inches from the heel a smart tap on the horse. As the blow is struck pull with both hands so as to separate the butt from the body. It may require more than one blow before the stock butt can be removed.

Note.—The blow should be struck over the shoulder of the horse and not on the outer end.

The rifle is now shifted to the 4th Position.

4TH POSITION. FIG. 5.

Clamped in a vice between the backsight and body, the sight being uppermost and raised as shown in Fig. 5.

In this position the following parts are removed :—

Bolt from body ; to do this, raise the knob of the bolt as far as it will go, and draw it back until the bolt head is brought up against the resisting shoulder, release the bolt head from its retaining spring with the thumb and forefinger of right hand, and rotate it upwards as far as it will go; now draw back the charger guide so as to clear the raised portion on the body, rotate the bolt head to the full extent and draw the bolt clear of the body.

Note.—With rifles having bridge charger guides the bolt head is rotated to the full extent in one motion, as there is no charger guide on the head to impede such movement.

Next remove screw, aperture, sight, spring; spring, aperture sight; locking bolt and safety catch, the last two being removed together. With the small drift remove " pin, fixing washer " of the axis pin of the back sight; washer; and with the large drift drive out the axis pin of leaf and remove the latter. The sight leaf spring, which is dovetailed in the sight bed, must be driven to the rear before it can be lifted out from the bed on removal of its fixing screw.

(To strip the bolt and backsights *see* p. 11.)

The rifle is now shifted to the 5th and final position.

5TH POSITION.   FIG. 6.

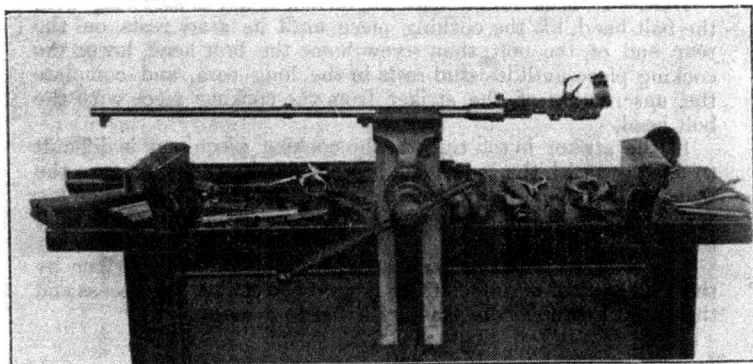

Clamped in a similar way to the 4th Position, but with the bed back sight downwards (*see* Fig. 6).

In this position the following parts are removed :—

With large screwdriver, the sear spring; with small screwdriver the sear screw, spring retaining bolt head and sear; then the cut-off screw and cut-off. If necessary drive out the axis pin of magazine catch and remove the latter.

To strip the Magazine.—Turn the stop clip down to the front (except No. 4 magazine), depress the rear end of the platform, and lift the front nut with the fingers of the right hand, turning the platform away from you, taking care to keep the rear side ears of the platform above the ribs of the case. Under no circumstances must leverage be applied to the lip of the platform at the front end to force it out. With point of screwdriver force off auxiliary spring.

To remove the platform spring slightly raise the clips on the under-side of the platform, which can then be drawn clear. This spring must not be removed unless absolutely necessary.

Note.—Care must be taken not to raise the clips more than is necessary to allow the rib on the spring to clear, as the clips are very liable to break off.

To strip the Bolt.—(1) With the small screwdriver remove the stop screw from charger guide, and slide the latter off.

(2) With the Implement Action, or Tool extractor spring, remove the extractor spring, using the punch end of the Implement to start the spring. With extractor screwdriver remove the axis screw and extractor.

(3) Unscrew the screw keeper striker (using a large screwdriver or coin) about four turns; see that stud on cocking piece is in the long cam, then with the bolt head unscrew the striker from the cocking piece, when the mainspring, striker, and cocking piece can be removed.

Note.—If it is found that the striker is not unscrewing with the bolt head, lift the cocking piece until its stud rests on the rear end of the bolt, then screw home the bolt head, lower the cocking piece until its stud rests in the long cam, and complete the unscrewing of the striker from the cocking piece with the bolt head.

If the striker is too tight in the cocking piece and is difficult to unscrew with the bolt head, fix the bolt in a vice, remove the bolt head and unscrew the striker with the " tool removing striker," using a large drift, or other convenient tool, as a tommy.

It should be remembered that when removing the striker by the bolt head, if too much force is used the striker lug recess and thread on tenon of bolt head are liable to damage.

Backsight. (*Except Mks. III and IV Rifles.*)

(1) The leaf having been removed, press in the catches of the slide and remove the latter from the leaf; the catches and springs may then be removed from the slide.

(2) Remove the fine-adjustment keeper screw, the fine-adjustment can then be removed from the leaf by turning the screw. Remove the two small springs from their recess in the rear face

of the dovetail on leaf; the fine adjustment screw and spring can now be removed.*

(3) Remove keeper plate of wind-gauge screw, unscrew the wind-gauge and remove it with its screw and spring. If necessary the screw, spring, sight leaf, and spring can be removed from the bed backsight on barrel.

Note.—The bed backsight, and the block, band foresight, on serviceable barrels should not be interfered with. The bed backsight, and block band foresight, are not interchangeable, being only suited for the barrel to which they are first fixed.

Backsight of Mk. III and Converted Mk. IV Rifles.

If it is only necessary to strip the sight, remove the hand-guards front and rear, without removing the nosecap; *i.e.*, remove the outer band, rear handguard, and slide the front handguard back clear of the nosecap and lift it off. If the rifle is being stripped down the same order will be observed in the case of the Mk. I, &c. In either case the rifle is secured in the 4th position.

To strip (1)—With driver-screw, fork, dial sight, remove the screw catch, slide, sight, back, with its spring.

(2) Drive out pin fixing washer, and remove the washer.

†(3) Drive out the pin axis backsight.

(4) Remove the leaf and take off the slide, depressing the catch, slide, backsight, so as to disengage the worm from the rack on the right side of leaf when so doing.

(5) Remove the catch with the worm fine adjustment.

(6) Drive out the pin, worm, fine adjustment, and remove the worm.

Note.—Only done when absolutely necessary.

(7) Drive out the pin, head, screw windgauge, and remove head, screw windgauge, with its spring.

Note.—This pin is tapered and care should be taken to drive it out the correct way.

(8) Unscrew screw windgauge, and remove the windgauge.

(9) Remove spring windgauge from the top of leaf.

Note.—The note above referring to beds, backsight, and block, band, foresight, applies to these rifles.

---

* In removing the fine-adjustment care should be taken to cover the springs, fine-adjustment, with the thumb of the left hand, as they are liable to fly out and get lost.

† The pins axis backsight of the Marks III and Converted Mk. IV short rifles are longer than those used with the other patterns of short rifles, owing to the increased width of the bed.

ASSEMBLING RIFLES SHORT, &c.

Positions in the vice.—The rifle is secured in the vice in positions similar to those employed for stripping, with the following exceptions, viz. :—

When placing a long " stock butt and stock bolt " the rifle is secured with the bed backsight down. With the rifle so placed it can be seen whether the bolt is in the correct position for the attachment of the fore-end, and for gauging the protrusion of the bolt through the face of the body.

Note.—If a stock butt is found to be loose, remove fore-end before tightening up the bolt, and if the protrusion of the stock-bolt is excessive, an additional washer for the stock-bolt must be used. The fore-end is always to be removed before, and replaced after, the stock butt.

To assemble backsight (*Mk. III and Convtd. Mk. IV*).

(1) Attach windgauge spring with the "T" portion on its shoulder at the top of leaf.

(2) Replace windgauge and its screw.

(3) Replace spring, screw, windgauge, with the thick or square edged nib in the slot prepared for it on the right side of windgauge.

(4) Replace head screw, windgauge, taking care that the tapered hole in head and screw coincide, and secure with its tapered pin.

(5) Replace worm fine-adjustment in the catch, slide, and drive home its axis pin. (This is a parallel pin.)

(6) Replace catch, with worm, in the slide.

*(7) Replace slide on leaf, worm to the same side as worm rack.

(8) Replace leaf on the bed backsight, and secure with its axis pin, driving latter home from L to R, using a pilot pin to give it a lead ; replace the washer and pin fixing.

(9) Replace spring catch slide, and screw catch, using the fork dial screw driver.

Backsight. (*Except Mks. III and IV.*)

(1) Replace the windgauge with its spring, screw, and keeper plate.

(2) Replace the fine adjustment screw and spring, and the two small spiral springs in their recesses on the leaf ; place the fine

---

* Whenever a large movement of the slide on the leaf is necessary, care must be taken to fully press home the catch so as to ensure the teeth on the worm clearing those on the rack. The teeth on the worm are case hardened, and are liable to break, or the rack may be damaged if this precaution is neglected.

adjustment on its dovetail and bring it home on the leaf by means of its screw, replace the keeper screw.

Note.—It will be necessary to keep the spiral springs compressed into their recesses (with the point of a large screw-driver) while the fine adjustment is being screwed home.

(3) Place the catches and springs in the slide and slip the latter over the axis end of leaf, keeping the catches fully compressed. When correctly assembled, the rounded edges of the opening on the top of slide should be next to the fine adjustment end of leaf.

Assembling other Components.

Bolt.—The striker should be screwed into the cocking-piece by the bolt head, as described in (1); the tool removing striker is *only* used when it is found impossible to do so by the bolt head.

(1) When using the bolt head place mainspring and striker in the bolt and screw home the bolt head about six turns, then place the cocking-piece in position, with its stud in the long cam, and screw home the bolt head. If the striker is not home in the cocking-piece raise the cocking piece and rest its stud on rear end of bolt, unscrew the bolt head about six turns, lower stud on the cocking-piece into long cam and complete the screwing home of the striker, replace the keeper screw and screw home the bolt head, with the stud on the cocking-piece in the short cam.

Replace extractor, screw and spring, replace charger guide (stop screw recess to the front) and stop screw, with the flat of latter flush with groove in charger guide.

When the bolt is correctly assembled gauge the striker point for protrusion and figure, by placing the stud on the cocking-piece in the long cam and using the Pattern " C " gauge, which gives the correct radius of point and measures the height, gauge the protrusion from ·04 in. to ·042 in.

(2) When using the tool removing striker place the main spring and striker in the bolt and the cocking-piece with its stud in the long cam, then with the " tool removing striker " screw home the striker in the cocking-piece until it is flush with the rear end of the latter, replace the striker keeper screw and screw home the bolt head, with the stud on cocking-piece in the short cam.

Magazine.—Replace spring of platform in the clips on the underside of the latter and close down the clips; replace the auxiliary spring in the case. See that stop clip is over to the front, replace the platform with spring, and turn up the stop clip.

Assembling the Rifle.

1st Position Assembling (5th Position Stripping).—Replace cut-off and cut-off screw (the head of the latter should be at least flush with the underside of the body), replace the sear, the spring retaining bolt head with its screw (and magazine catch and pin if removed) and the sear spring. A convenient method of re-

18

placing the latter is as follows:—Engage the long arm of the spring with the notch below the axis hole of the sear, then with the point of a large screwdriver applied to the nib on the other arm of spring, push the latter gently down until it engages the notch on the magazine catch. Another method:—Engage long arm of spring as before, then with the point of the large screwdriver placed between the bight, or arms of spring, twist the screwdriver so that the short branch moves down and engages with the magazine catch. The former method is preferable, as there is less likelihood of straining the spring.

The rifle is now shifted to the 2nd Position (4th Position Stripping).

2nd Position.—Replace the spring sight leaf and its fixing screw, replace the backsight leaf (having correctly assembled the slide) compressing the spring and passing the axis pin through from L to R, using the pilot pin to give the necessary lead; replace the washer and pin fixing, seeing that the tapered holes coincide and that the pin is in the vertical point down.

Next assemble the safety catch on the locking bolt as follows:—Place the catch on the stem of the bolt, so that a line marked on the face of the former is parallel to the flat at end of the latter, engage the screw threads and screw home; if correctly assembled the top end of catch should then be nearly in line with rear end of bolt (catch and bolt should be in the relative positions of the hands of a clock at eleven o'clock). It may be necessary to try a few times before the correct threads engage. Replace aperture sight, spring, and screw spring aperture sight.

Replace the bolt as follows:—See that the cocking-piece and resisting lug are in a straight line and that the *bolt head is screwed home.** Place the bolt in the ribway of the body, engaging the head with the extractor upwards, push the bolt forward until the head is just clear of the resisting shoulder, turn the bolt head down to the right, push the charger guide forward (except Mks. III and IV) and press the bolt head over its retaining spring, close the breach and press the sear.

Remove the Rifle from the vice and insert the stock butt in the body, and tap it home with the heel of the hand. If any difficulty is experienced in getting the butt home use the " Anvil stock butt " and drive it home as follows:—Grasp the body with the left hand, muzzle pointing downwards, then insert the " Anvil " so that it lies evenly on the butt, and with a hammer held in the right hand drive the butt home by striking the Anvil squarely.

Now shift to the 3rd Position (3rd Position Stripping), but

* Particular attention should be paid to this whenever the bolt is removed from the body, as now there is no bolt cover the bolt head is at liberty to turn. If not screwed home the assembled bolt is lengthened, and when replaced in the body in this condition a jam occurs when loading.
This applies to charger loading rifles also.

with the toe of the butt upwards and backsight down. Pass the "stock bolt" up through the butt and with the brace and bit screw it home fairly tight; now gauge the protrusion with gauge supplied and see that it lies within the maximum and minimum limits,* and is squarely in the vertical so as to correctly engage with the keeper plate in the fore-end. Remove the bit and insert a wad stock bolt, pushing it home with the bit. Replace the butt plate and screws.

Now shift the Rifle to the 4th Position (2nd Position Stripping). Assemble the component parts of the fore-end, viz.:—Dial sight plate, dial sight plate fixing screw, dial pointer, spring and pivot screw. See that the stock bolt keeper plate is placed in its recess in the fore-end with the bevelled edges inwards; shift the inner band to the approximate position it will occupy when the fore-end is in position; place the spring and stud in the fore-end, and the latter on the barrel, taking care that the keeper plate is engaging with the square end of " stock bolt," and also that a screwed boss on the inner band is directly under the hole prepared for it in the fore-end.

Now place the drift fore-end (wood) in the trigger guard recess with its slot bearing against the magazine catch, and with a hammer drive the fore-end home on the barrel. Next replace the inner band screw and spring, raise the backsight, replace the nose-cap, tapping it gently home; place the hand guards front and rear in position, replace trigger guard with its screws front and rear, screwing each down a few turns alternately, and magazine; place the outer band in position and shift the Rifle to the 5th position.

In the 5th Position (1st Position Stripping) replace the screws nose-cap, front and rear, and the outer band swivel screw. After the latter has been replaced it should be expanded with a centre punch to prevent it jarring loose.

Note.—The long side of swivels should be on the right or opposite side to the aperture and dial sights, so that the sling will not interfere with the sighting when using these sights.

When all the parts are correctly assembled the various springs should be weighed as detailed later.

---

* If the stock bolt should protrude more than the limit laid down, it can be adjusted by adding an additional stock bolt washer, adjusted, if necessary, to a suitable thickness, under the head of the stock bolt.

STRIPPING RIFLES CHARGER LOADING, M.L.E.

These rifles are secured in six different positions during stripping and assembling; the tools used are, with one or two exceptions, the same as those used with the short rifles.

1st Position.—Fixed in the vice between the backsight and body, sight uppermost and muzzle pointing towards the left. In this position the following parts are removed, viz. :—

(1) The hand guard (using the tool removing if necessary).

(2) The safety catch, spring and pin. The screw keeper striker is also removed in this position as it is the most convenient.

To remove the safety catch proceed as follows :—

Fully cock the striker, raise the safety catch to a mid-way position (easing the cocking-piece if difficulty is experienced in doing so), then with a drift drive out the safety catch, ease the cocking-piece forward by hand, remove the bolt from body, turn up the bolt and safety pin and spring will drop out.

(3) Remove extractor spring, screw, and extractor.

(4) Remove the bolt head.

(5) With "tool removing" unscrew the striker from the cocking-piece and remove mainspring and cocking-piece.

The rifle is now shifted to the 2nd Position :—Clamped at the band lower, muzzle to the right and guard uppermost. In this position remove the following :—

(1) The magazine.

(2) The magazine platform and spring.

(3) Remove screw nose-cap, and slide the nose-cap along the barrel. This component cannot be taken off the barrel unless the screw protector fore-sight, protector, and blade fore-sight have been previously removed, an operation which may be carried out only by an armourer, as it will necessitate a re-adjustment of the sighting.

(The front of the fore-sight block and the blade fore-sight will in future manufacture be lined to ensure the blade fore-sight being returned to the position originally adjusted after testing and passing for shooting, when it is found necessary to remove the blade.)

4. Remove screw band lower, swivel, and lower band, sliding the latter along the fore-end and barrel as with the nose-cap.

Now shift to the 3rd Position :—Clamped at the parallel portion of butt, muzzle to the right and guard uppermost. Remove the following :—

(1) Front and back screws of guard, and guard.

(2) Raise aperture sight and remove the fore-end.

(3) Remove dial sight screw and dial sight.

Now shift the rifle to the 4th Position:—Clamped at the parallel portion of butt, the backsight uppermost and muzzle pointing towards the left.

In this position remove the following:—

(1) Butt plate and strap screws, butt plate, wad, stock bolt, and stock butt.

Now shift to the 5th Position :—Clamped in a similar position to that of the 1st, but with the woodwork removed. In this position remove:—

(1) Aperture sight spring screw, spring, and aperture sight.

Now shift to the 6th Position :—Clamped between backsight and body, sight downwards. Remove the following:--

(1) Cut-off screw and cut-off.

(2) Sear spring.

(3) Sear screw, sear, and bolt head retaining spring.

(4) Magazine catch pin and catch.

Stripping the Backsight (special instruction only).—If it should be considered necessary to strip this component it will be found that the most convenient position for the rifle will be the 1st position as above. To strip the sight proceed as follows :—

(1) Release the clamping nut, raise the leaf to a vertical position and remove screw stop and slide from the leaf.

(2) Remove clamping nut and stud (not No. 2 slide).

(3) Remove the pin fixing and head screw windgauge (using the drift pin, fixing washer, backsight, R.S.M.L.E.). This pin is tapered.

(4) Remove screw windgauge (using the driver screw extractor axis), windgauge and spring windgauge from box on slide (and clamping nut and stud if No. 2 slide).

(5) Remove the spring slide backsight by springing its rounded end clear of the shoulder on the face of slide.

(6) Drive out the pin axis backsight and remove the leaf.

To Assemble the Backsight.—(1) Replace the leaf and axis pin.

(2) Replace spring slide (and clamping stud and nut if No. 2 slide) and spring windgauge (in its box on the slide with the convex side up), and the windgauge.

(3) Replace the screw windgauge and screw it home.

(4) Replace the head screw windgauge and pin, taking care that the tapered holes in screw and head coincide.

(5) Replace clamping stud and nut and screw home the clamping nut, taking care that the helical projection on the nut is to the rear of the stud (not No. 2 slide).

(6) Replace the slide on the leaf.

Note.—The inside edge or surface of the stud must be below or at least flush with the inside surface of the slide to clear and allow of replacement.

(7) Replace screw, stop, slide, sight, back.

ASSEMBLING RIFLES CHARGER LOADING, M. L. E.

The rifles are secured in similar positions as for stripping, with the same exception as in the case of the short rifles *re* the "Stock butt and stock bolt."

Proceed as follows :—Having assembled the backsight as already detailed, secure the rifle in the 1st Position (6th Position Stripping).

(1) Replace magazine catch and catch pin.

(2) Sear, spring retaining bolt head, and sear screw.

(3) Sear spring (as detailed for Short Rifle).

(4) Cut-off and cut-off screw.

Now shift to the 2nd Position.

2nd Position (5th Position Stripping).

Replace aperture sight, spring and aperture sight spring screw.

Now shift to the 3rd Position.

3rd Position (4th Position Stripping, but with the backsight down so as to be able to gauge the protrusion of the stock bolt).

Replace the stock butt, stock bolt, seeing that it is within the Max^m and Min^m limits* (using the gauge supplied) and squarely in the vertical, turn rifle so that sight is uppermost and replace the wad, butt plate, butt plate and strap screws.

Now shift to the 4th Position,

4th Position (3rd Position Stripping).

(1) Replace in its recess in the fore-end the dial sight plate and screw home the dial sight screw.

(2) Replace dial sight pointer, spring, and screw dial sight pivot.

(3) Replace the stock fore-end, using the drift fore-end and hammer to drive it home.

Note.—Care must be taken that the keeper plate is in position and the stock bolt squarely in the vertical.

(4) Replace the guard, seeing that the trigger engages with the sear ; replace back and front guard screws, screwing each down alternately.

Now shift to the 5th Position.

5th Position (2nd Position Stripping).

(1) Replace the lower band with its swivel and screw.

(2) Replace the nose-cap, tapping it home with the drift fore-end and a hammer, replace the screw nose-cap.

---

* If the bolt should protrude more than the limit laid down it can be adjusted by adding an additional stock bolt washer, adjusted, if necessary, to a suitable thickness, under the head of the stock bolt.

(3) Replace in the magazine the magazine auxiliary spring, platform and spring, and turn up the stop clip.

(4) Replace the magazine in the rifle, and see that it is properly secured by its catch.

Now shift the rifle to the 6th Position.

6th Position (1st Position Stripping).

Assemble the bolt as follows :—

(1) Replace the cocking-piece on the bolt with the stud in the long cam, drop in the mainspring and striker, and with "tool removing" screw home the striker until it is flush with the rear end of the cocking-piece, and secure with its keeper screw.

(2) Screw home the bolt head* in the bolt.

(3) Replace the extractor, screw, and spring in the bolt head and replace the bolt in the rifle.

(4) Replace the safety catch as follows :—

(a) Fully cock the striker. (b) Drop in the spring and pin. (c) Hold the safety catch in the mid-way position and drive it home with the hammer, then lower the catch and pull the trigger.

(5) Replace the handguard.

---

* See footnote on page 18.

ACTION OF MECHANISM—MAGAZINE RIFLES.

Assuming that the rifle has just been fired, there are four distinct motions of the bolt necessary before another round is ready to be fired.

(1) *Raising the Bolt Lever.*—The bolt is revolved, but the cocking piece and bolt head are prevented from turning, the former by the groove in the body, the latter by its hook engaging the rib on the body. Consequently the cam-shaped face between the long and short grooves of the bolt bears against the stud on the cocking-piece, and forces the cocking-piece to the rear, thus withdrawing the striker from the cartridge and slightly compressing the mainspring from the front. At the same time the sloping face of the recess in the body bears against the sloping face of the bolt lug, and the bolt is drawn back with a powerful motion, the extractor moves in and engages with the cartridge and primary extraction of the cartridge is effected. The long rib on the bolt is now opposite the rib-way in the body, and the stud on the cocking-piece is in the short groove.

(2) *Drawing back the Bolt.*—The cartridge is extracted and ejected by the action of the shallowing groove and ejector screw on the left side of the body. The bolt is brought up by the projection on the bolt head coming against the resistance shoulder of the body.

(3) *Pushing forward the Bolt.*—The head of the bolt engages with the top cartridge from the magazine or with the round placed in by hand, and pushes it into the chamber. The full bent on the cocking-piece engages with the sear, and the mainspring is compressed from the rear. The stud between the grooves on the bolt passes clear in front of the stud on the cocking-piece.

(4) *Turning down the Bolt Lever.*—The bolt lug and the long rib, engaging respectively with the sloping recess in the body and the resistance shoulder, force the bolt forward against the base of the cartridge. The cartridge is now firmly supported, the mainspring is fully compressed, the action is at full cock, and the stud on the cocking-piece is opposite the long groove in the bolt.

Pressing the Trigger.

The sear is revolved, at first with a slower and more powerful motion and then with a quicker motion, the bents are disengaged, and the striker flies forward and fires the cartridge.

(The charger loading rifle has only one motion in the pull-off instead of a double motion action).

Safety Arrangements.

(1) Locking bolt and safety-catch.

To prevent the rifle being fired accidentally.

(2) Studs on cocking-piece and rear end of bolt, and half or safety-bent in locking piece engaging on sear.

To prevent the rifle being fired with the bolt not properly closed.

In this case, either (*a*) the stud on cocking-piece coming against sloping face of stud on bolt, automatically closes the bolt ; or (*b*) stud on cocking-piece strikes full against stud on bolt. If the bolt is then closed, the sear engages in the half-bent, and the action is locked, as the two studs are side by side. The action must be re-cocked by pulling back the cocking-piece by hand.

WEIGHING OF SPRINGS.

Method of Weighing.—A spring balance, called a "Tester, trigger, pull" (T.T.P.), is supplied for the purpose of weighing all the springs, upon the correctness of which, in conjunction with cleanliness of the parts, depends the accurate and smooth working of the breech action. If a vice is available it should be used in preference to any other arrangement, as more accurate results are obtained. Once the rifle is fixed in the vice, its position need not be changed, as all the springs can be weighed in that position as described below.

Position in the Vice.—Remove the handguard, rear, so as not to split it with the jaws of the vice.

Secure the rifle immediately in rear of the bed backsight, in a horizontal position, the muzzle pointing towards the left, and the right side up.

Note.—The magazine must always be in position.

Now fully cock the mechanism and proceed as follows.

Pull off.—(The pressure required to release the sear from the full bent of cocking-piece.)

Place the friction roller of the T.T.P. over the finger piece of the trigger, and holding the other end in the right hand, pull in a line diagonally across the small of the butt, steadying the right hand on the back of the left, the finger tips of latter resting on the butt near the heel.

A steady pull should be given, and when the trigger begins to move the weight should be from 3 to 4 lbs.; continue the pull, and when the striker is released the balance should show 5 to 6 lbs. (Rifles short, double pull.)

Charger Loading Rifles.—Pull to move trigger when mainspring is eased $3\frac{1}{2}$ to $4\frac{1}{2}$ lbs., pull off 5 to 7 lbs. (Single pull.)

Note.—The above results are only obtained when the components of the action, including the trigger, are clean and free from oil, or other matter, causing obstruction.* The action should, therefore, be thoroughly cleaned, and slightly oiled; special attention being paid to the following:—(1) That the mainspring is the correct weight. (2) That the bent on the cocking-piece and the ribs on the trigger (short rifles) have not been damaged. (3) That there is no packing or foreign substance on the sear seat in the body. (4) That the sear screw is not bent.

---

* The action may appear free from oil, but if there is an accumulation of dirty or thick oil in the mainspring chamber, in the bolt hole of the cocking-piece, or in striker hole in the bolt head, miss-fires are likely to occur.

If all these points have been attended to and it is still found that the weight is outside the limits laid down, the rifle should be returned to store for special examination.

Mainspring.—(1) With the striker in the fired position, place the tag of the T.T.P. over the end of the cocking-piece, and pull in a direct line with the bolt. When the cocking-piece moves the weight should be from 7 to 9 lbs. (2) Cock the action test again in a similar way, when the weight should be from 14 to 16 lbs.

Spring retaining Bolt Head.—(1) Draw back the bolt until the head is over the spring retaining. (2) Place the claws of tag round the bolt head, and pull with the T.T.P. slightly above the horizontal, and at right angles to the bolt ; when the bolt head is released from the spring the weight should be from 10 to 16 lbs. If the weight is outside these limits examine the sear screw and see if it is home and tight.

Extractor Spring.—With the bolt head released, as by the last operation, place the tip of one of the claws of T.T.P. under the hook of the extractor and pull against its spring; when the extractor moves the weight should be from 4½ to 5½ lbs. or in the case of rifles having the new pattern spring (which can be identified by the Fig. 3 stamped on the inside of the long arm) from 7 to 9 lbs.

Trap Butt Spring.—Place the tip of the claw under the nib of trap butt; to move the latter the weight should be from 2 to 3 lbs. (converted rifles, and rifles charger loading, 3½ to 4½ lbs.).

Extraction, Ejection, and Magazine Spring.—Having weighed all the springs as detailed above, charge the magazine with 10 dummy cartridges fed from chargers ; close and open the cut-off to see if it works freely ; work the action by closing and opening the breech, see that the magazine feeds correctly, that primary extraction takes place and that the bolt works freely and ejects correctly. If the magazine does not feed correctly, strip and examine it for dents, or other damage, and if necessary replace the platform spring.

Note.—To ensure that the "ejection" is correct, it will be necessary to try the action with *empty cartridge cases*, loading the cases separately by hand.

MISS-FIRES AND FAILURES.

Assuming that the ammunition is good, these may be placed under the following headings, viz. :—

A. Miss-fires.
B. Non-Extraction or Bad Ejection.
C. Light or Heavy pull-off.
D. Defective Magazine Supply.

A. Miss-fires.—Probably due to :—(1) Rusty, weak, or broken mainspring. (2) Bent or broken striker. (3) Insufficient protrusion, owing to (*a*) point of striker worn, (*b*) striker screwed too far into cocking-piece, (*c*) rust or grit in front of striker, or damaged hole in bolt head, (*d*) striker having turned in the cocking-piece, (*e*) wrong pattern keeper screw, viz., a M.L.M. screw in a M.L.E. cocking-piece, (*f*) stud on cocking-piece or long groove in bolt burred up,(*g*) thick or dirty oil in mainspring chamber, in striker hole in bolt head, or in bolt hole of cocking piece. (4) Bolt not properly closed. (5) Bolt or body badly worn or indented at recoil shoulders.

B. Non-Extraction or Bad Ejection.—Probably due to :—(1) Rusty, dirty, or scored chamber. (2) Broken extractor, weak or broken extractor spring. (3) Hook of extractor worn. (4) Extractor screw hole enlarged or screw worn small. (5) Ejector screw worn. (6) Wrong pattern of extractor spring. (7) Bolt head very loose in bolt. (8) Dirty or rusty chamber.

C. Light Pull-off. Probably due to :—(1) Light mainspring. (2) Light sear spring. (3) Dirt or packing on the sear seat. (4) Striker not screwed home. (5) Sear too low, or the magazine not in position. (6) Improper form of bent of cocking-piece.

Heavy Pull-off.—Probaby due to :—(1) Main or sear spring too heavy. (2) Sear too high. (3) A bent sear screw. (4) Magazine not pushed home to the correct position, *i.e.*, the bent on the magazine catch not engaging with the bent on the magazine case, and consequently the sear spring unduly compressed. (5) Improper form of bent of cocking-piece.

D. Defective Magazine Supply.—Generally due to :—(1) Platform spring weak or broken. (2) Distorted platform. (3) Magazine case dented or rusted. (4) Magazine not engaged by the catch. (5) Damaged cartridges.

Inaccurate Shooting.

As far as the rifle is concerned, this would be due probably to some of the following causes :—

(1) Front or back sight not correctly adjusted or sight slide wrongly assembled (reversed).

(2) Badly rusted or enlarged bore.

(3) Bent, bulged or dented barrel.

(4) Warped fore-end or handguard.

(5) Fore-end or nose-cap incorrectly adjusted.

(6) Wrong bolt.

With regard to (5), the fore-end and nose-cap are carefully adjusted to each rifle, and play of ·002″ is allowed between the barrel and nose-cap, and between the barrel and inner band. The nose-cap and fore-end are both given the same number as the rifle.

With regard to (6), the bolt is carefully adjusted to each rifle, and given the same number as the rifle. Bolts must always be used with the particular rifle to which they are numbered for the following reasons :—The shock on discharge is taken up by the longitudinal rib on the bolt, supported by the resistance shoulder, and at the same time by the lug on the underside of the bolt, supported by the rear-wall of the oblique cutting in the body. Therefore if the stock of discharge is not evenly divided between these two supports, the shooting will be erratic ; the shot going towards the right or left according to which side takes the greater part of the shock.

EXAMINATION OF SHORT AND CHARGER LOADING RIFLES.

The following points should be attended to when carrying out the examination of the above rifles, using the ordinary gauges supplied to armourers.

Take the rifle in the hands and commence at the nose-cap working back towards the butt, and note the following :—

(1) That the numbers on bolt, body, nose-cap, fore-end, barrel, and sight leaf coincide. (Nose-cap and fore-end are numbered in short rifles only.)

(2) That there are no parts deficient.

(3) That all screws are home and fast, the outer or lower band screws not being too tightly screwed up.

Note.—Swivel and band screws go in from left to right.

(4) Remove the bolt and gauge the height and form of striker (as detailed on *p.* 17). See that the striker is not screwed too far into the cocking-piece, that the nut or screw keeper striker is. in the correct position, and that the charger guide is not over loose but works freely. Examine the extractor and its screw as to wear, and see that the bolt head is screwed home.

(5) That the sear nose engages in the half and full bents on the cocking-piece, and that it clears the lug on the bolt.

(6) That the action works freely, extracts, and ejects cartridges and empty cartridge cases properly.

(7) That the barrel, particularly the chamber, is free from dirt, rust, cuts, excessive scoring, or other damage.

(8) That the sword-bayonet fits properly on the sword-bar of the nose-cap, the spring acts on the sword bolt, and that the bayonet is correct in all respects (*see* note at end).

(9) That the front and back sights are in good condition, the leaf is firm at its joint, the fine adjustment and windgauge move smoothly and fit firmly, the slide moves smoothly and the catches engage truly in the racks, that the slide is correctly assembled on the leaf and the ramps are not damaged. With Mk. III and converted Mk. IV that the worm teeth are not damaged, and engage truly with the rack when the catch is released.

(10) With Mk. III and converted Mk. IV that the "Protector backsight" has the chequered edges towards the breech or its cranked wing on the right, to permit of extreme right traverse to the windgauge.

(11) That the aperture and dial sights are not bent or damaged and work smoothly.

Note.—In particular that the dial sight plate is of the correct pattern. (All short rifles will have the same pattern plate for future manufacture and for spare.)

(12) That the magazine is working properly, and is not dented, that the platform rises freely when fully loaded with 10 dummy cartridges, and that the cut-off works freely.

(13) Remove handguards and examine the fore-end for rust in the barrel edges.

(14) See that the stock butt is firmly attached to the body.

(15) Weigh all springs as detailed.

(16) See that the inner band spring is free (using the point of large screwdriver); if it sticks, it is generally due to an excess of wood.

(17) See that the spring stud fore-end is free (place the point of a bullet in the bore and rock, when there should be a slight movement). The barrel should always bear against the top of the elliptical opening in the nose-cap.

(18) See that the bolt closes over the ·064" gauge, and fails to do so with the ·074".

Note.—If it closes over the ·074" gauge the rifle must be returned for special inspection and adjustment.

(19) See that the striker works easily in the bolt. To do this close the breech and ease the striker, place the thumb of right hand on the knob of lever, and press the trigger with the fore-finger; then with the thumb and forefinger of left pull the cocking-piece backward and forward. Note if the stud on cocking-piece is rubbing against the walls of the long cam. If so, the rifle must be returned to store for adjustment (this defect would probably cause a miss-fire).

(20) See that the safety arrangements are in correct working order. To ascertain this proceed as follows :—(1) Turn the safety catch to the rear and see if the bolt is safely locked, turn to the front and fully cock by opening and closing the breech. (2) Try the safety catch in this position, now place the locking bolt in the mid-way position and press the trigger, when the striker should hang up, now push the safety bolt fully to the firing position; this should release the striker, and as the cocking-piece moves to the front the sear nose should engage with the safety bent.

Note.—If this action takes place correctly it shows that the sear is standing at its proper angle, and also that there is no danger of premature firing owing to worn full cock bents.

Sword Bayonet.—The sword bayonet when properly fitted should have the bolt in the pommel flush with the exterior of the pommel, and the bolt engaging truly with its bearings on the standard, or sword bar of the nose-cap. Should the bolt project beyond the pommel, whether fixed or unfixed, it indicates that grit or dirt has accumulated in the bolt hole, or lodged upon the shoulder bearings for the bolt in the pommel; the sword bayonet would be thereby prevented from being firmly fixed or locked. If the bolt is flush with the pommel when unfixed, and projects when fixed, the end of the pommel is probably bearing on the nose-cap in the case of sword bayonets pattern 1888, and in the case of sword bayonets pattern 1903 and 1907 on the rounded end of the sword bar of nose-cap and bolt of bayonet. This would cause the sword bayonet to be loose, and liable to drop off. This defect should be attended to by an armourer.

TESTING BORE OF BARRELS FOR WEAR.

Before applying the gauges, see that the barrel is thoroughly cleaned and free from metallic fouling, bulges, cuts, or bends. The ·303″ plug should then run through the bore. The barrels are sentenced as unserviceable if—(1) ·307″ plug runs through, or (2) ·308″ plug enters muzzle ·25″ (*i.e.*, to line on plug), or (3) ·310″ plug enters breech ·25″ (*i.e.*, rear end of plug is flush with rear end of barrel), or (4) the No. 2 lead plug enters breech ·5″ (*i.e.*, rear end of plug is flush with rear end of barrel).

The measurements at breech end will be taken, in the case of Magazine arms, from the face of barrel, and in M.M. and M.E. arms from the bottom of the cartridge head recess.

Note.—In a new or slightly worn barrel the rear end of the ·310″ plug does not enter to the line indicating the commencement of the toleration as the front end is checked by the lead at ·3″ to the rear of the commencement of the bore which the plug is intended to gauge. The lead is conicle, and gradually decreases in diameter to ·303″.

Reference gauges are kept at A.O.D. stations to periodically check those used by armourers by comparison with the reference gauges in worn barrels, etc. The reference gauges are stamped " REFERENCE," in addition to the usual marking.

Sentencing Cord-Worn Barrels. (*See* Appendix XXV, R.A.O.S.)

To determine the serviceability of a cord-worn barrel, the following points should be observed :—

(*a*) A barrel will be considered unserviceable through cord wear at breech end when the *fired case* shows clear signs of having *expanded into the cord groove.*

(*b*) If the wear exists at the muzzle, barrels should, if possible, be practically tested for accuracy, as laid down in M.R., 1909. If a 500 yards range is not available, the rifle should be fired at 100 feet range, when the centres of the best 9 out of 10 shots should fall within a circle 1·75 inches in diameter.

Note.—Cord wear in barrels is caused by the pull-through cord rubbing against the breech or muzzle end of the barrel when the pull-through is not drawn through the barrel in line with the bore. The friction ultimately cuts a groove which may lead to burst cases when it occurs at the breech end, and destroys accuracy when it occurs at the muzzle.

(B 10030)   C

Explanation of Various Marks on Rifles.

Mark.	Where Found.	Meaning.
E.Y. ...	Butt, fore-end, body, barrel and bolt.	May be utilized in case of emergency.
D.P.	Ditto	For drill purposes.
M.T.	Ditto	For use with Morris tube.
A.T.	Ditto	For use with ·22-inch tube and ·22-inch rim-fire cartridge.
	Marks on Barrel.	
Year of manufacture.	Underneath Knox form.	
Rotation number and series letter.	On right of Knox form.	
P.	Left of Knox form ...	Parallel bore.
✸	Front of Knox form ...	Rust or cut inside barrel.
✶	On other positions of the barrel.	Erosion or rust on exterior of barrel near the star.
W̊. ...	Left side of Knox form, at front end of reinforce for muzzle, and rear end for breech.	Cord-worn.
R. ...	Knox form	Found rusty by viewer and to be cleaned by armourer.
ℛℛ ...	Knox form	A.I. departmental mark.
E. ...	Knox form	Enfield rifling. Will be discontinued.
⊛ ...	Same as ✶ ...	If marked by A.O.D., to distinguish from R.S.A.F. marking.
(W̊) ...	Same as W̊. ...	Cord-worn if marked by A.O.D.

Also various proof and manufacturing marks will be found on the barrel.

Marks on body.

Manufacturer s initials and place of manufacture Mark of rifle Year of manufacture	On right side, close to the stock butt. In converted rifles on the left side.
Rotation number and series letter.	On right side, close to the barrel.

Various proof and inspection marks.

Marks on other components.

Mark.	Where Found.	Meaning.
Rotation number and series letter.—	Bolt, fore-end, nose-cap, and sight-leaf.—	
S. ...	Fore-end ...	Early patterns of short rifles. Fitted with spring and stud.
2 ...	Right of butt ...	Early patterns. Plate keeper stock bolt in fore-end.
P. ...	Right of butt ...	Early patterns. Compressed butt.
S. ...	On stock-butt ...	Short butt, 12 inches.
L. ...	On stock-butt ...	Long butt, 13 inches.

Note.—A star on the left side of the top strap of a pistol denotes that cut or rust may be found inside.

A star on the pommel of a sword-bayonet denotes that the pommel is blemished.

Carbines and rifles issued on payment are marked with a special mark before issue from Weedon.

SWORD BAYONETS.

There are five patterns of sword bayonets in use with magazine arms, viz. :—

    Pattern 1888.   Marks I, II, and III.   For long rifles.
        „   1903.   Mark I.   ...   „ short „
        „   1907.   „   „   „   „

The various marks of the 1888 pattern differ only in small details.

The 1903 pattern differs from the 1888 pattern in having the ring of the cross-piece and the mortice on the same side. It has a larger nut and stronger bolt.

The 1907 pattern differs from previous patterns in having the blade five inches longer and single edged, with lightening grooves to bring it down to about the same weight as previous patterns. One end of the cross-piece is hooked.

The approximate weight of the above sword-bayonets is 16½ ozs.

The scabbards of 1888 and 1903 patterns are interchangeable for patterns 1888 and 1903 sword-bayonets. The 1907 scabbard is special to the 1907 bayonet.

WEBLEY PISTOL.

Five patterns may be met with in the service, viz. :—Marks I, I*, II, III, IV.   Some of the latter Mark are provided with 6-inch barrels for the use of officers and cadets.

The Webley pistol was introduced in August, 1890, to supersede the Enfield pattern.   It consists of (i) the barrel, (ii) the body, (iii) the cylinder.

The barrel is connected to the body by a knuckle joint and strap with spring lock.   The body is slotted out to form seatings and bearings for the various parts of the breech action, and is provided with vulcanite grips in place of the wooden grips of the Enfield pistols.   The cylinder has chambers for six cartridges, and is pivoted on a tubular axis attached to the barrel.   The extractor works in this axis, surrounded by a spiral spring, and is actuated by a lever carried in the knuckle joint.

Calibre, ·441 inch.
Weight, 2 lbs. 3 ozs.
Rifling, 7 grooves, 1 turn in 20 calibres, right-handed.
Muzzle velocity, 715 f.s.
Sighted up to 50 yards.

TO STRIP WEBLEY PISTOL, MARKS III AND IV.

The small screwdriver and cramps, as a rule, will be found sufficient; it may be necessary to use the vice if the screws are very tight, in that case the pistol should be clamped either by the barrel (taking care not to damage fore-sight) or body with stocks removed.

To strip.—(1) Remove stock screw and lift off stocks left and right.

(2) Unscrew and remove trigger guard screws and lift off the guard.

(3) Lift by hand the mainspring stud out of its recess in the body, then fully cock the hammer, pass the fork of cramp over both branches of mainspring and slip it along towards the hammer as far as possible, now release the hammer by pressing the trigger; the spring is now held in compression by the cramp and can be lifted out from the body.

(4) Lift out mainspring auxiliary.

(5) Unscrew trigger screw and take out the trigger with pawl, the latter can then be lifted off.

(6) Unscrew hammer screw and lift out the hammer.

(7) Unscrew cam lever fixing screw, release barrel catch and open the pistol to the fullest extent, now push cam lever towards the cylinder, see that "Cam Cylinder" drops clear of the "Cylinder," when the latter can be lifted clear of its axis. Unscrew "Cam Lever" screw and lift out "Cam Lever."

(8) Unscrew joint axis screw and tap out joint axis pin towards the left, remove barrel from body and extractor lever from barrel.

(9) Slip cramp over the barrel catch spring so as to take the pressure off the catch, then remove screw, the barrel catch, slide the cramp off spring and remove the latter.

(10) Remove screws cam cylinder and lift off the cam cylinder.

To strip cylinder.—Unscrew nut extractor (with a small drift or Tommy) and lift out extractor and spring.

To strip hammer.—(1) Remove screw swivel hammer and lift out swivel.

(2) Remove screw catch hammer and lift the catch and spiral spring out from its recess.

To strip trigger.—Remove screw, spring, stop trigger, and lift out spring and stop.

If necessary remove screw fixing shield and tap ladder out to one side of its dovetail.

If necessary drive out "axis pin" of swivel butt and remove latter.

(Replace above in the Reverse Order.)

Examination of Webley Pistols.

The following points should be attended to when examining Webley pistols:—

(1) That there are no parts deficient.

(2) That rotation number on barrel, body, and cylinder coincide (other components have the last three numbers of rotation numbers).

(3) That all screws are home and fast.

(4) That all parts fit and work properly, special attention being directed to the following:—

> (a) Cylinder should not have more than ·004-inch rotary movement on its axis with the trigger pressed.
>
> (b) That the cylinder revolves freely in the loading position.
>
> (c) That the "full-cock" bents are in good condition.
>
> (d) That the cylinder chambers and bore are free from rust, cuts, excessive scoring, or other damage.
>
> (e) That the extractor is working properly—*extracts* and *ejects* freely.
>
> (f) That the lifting point of pawl and ratchet teeth are not damaged or unduly worn.
>
> (g) Gauge the protrusion of point—·044-inch to ·054-inch.
>
> (h) Gauge distance of face of body to cylinder—·052-inch.
>
> (i) See that trigger catch, cylinder stop, and hammer stop are working correctly.
>
> (j) Weigh all springs as follows:—
>
>> (1) *Pull-off.*—Clamp the pistol in a vice by its barrel, and full-cock, apply T.T.P. to trigger. To release hammer a power of 6 to 8 lbs. is required.
>>
>> (2) *Trigger action.*—With hammer in fired position the pull on trigger to raise the hammer to full-cock—12 to 15 lbs.
>>
>> (3) *Mainspring.*—Keeping trigger firmly pressed by finger so that hammer face bears on pistol body, apply the T.T.P. to a loop of twine passed over the head of hammer, and pull in direction of axis of barrel; the weight to move it—3¾ to 4¼ lbs.
>>
>> (4) *Barrel catch spring.*—Apply the tags on T.T.P. to the front top of catch and pull horizontally to the rear. The weight should be from 4 to 6 lbs.

Miss-fires with Webley Pistols.

May be caused by the following:—

> (i) Short nose to hammer.
>
> (ii) Hammer striking cap high low, to the right, or left.
>
> (iii) Weak mainspring.
>
> (iv) Barrel catch not quite home.

Note.—The above may be remedied :—

    (i) By filing away a little of the shoulder of the hammer or replace by spare part.

    (ii) May be caused by backward or forward movement of cylinder on its axis, or excessive rotary movement on the axis due to worn ratchet teeth or lifting point of pawl. Replace defective part.

    (iii) Replace by spare component.

    (iv) Examine spring and catch, see that the axis screw is not over tight, or replace defective part by spare one.

Pistol Webley.—Action of Mechanism.

(*a*) *Cocking by hand.*—On pulling the hammer to the rear, the toe of the hammer catches under the trigger-nose and raises the rear end of the trigger, thus lowering the trigger catch and gradually raising the trigger stop and the pawl. The pawl, engaging the ratchet teeth on the extractor, revolves the cylinder one-sixth of a turn. The cylinder is checked in the correct position by the trigger stop and is locked by the trigger catch. The trigger-nose falls into the bent on the toe of the hammer, and the mainspring is now fully compressed, from the top by the action of the hammer swivel, from the bottom by the upward movement of the mainspring auxiliary.

On *pulling the trigger* the bents are disengaged, the hammer falls and fires the cartridge.

On *releasing the trigger* the mainspring auxiliary, acted on by the mainspring, presses down the pawl and trigger-nose, and its projection engaging with the heel of the hammer, it makes the hammer revolve to the rear and thus causes the rebound action, withdrawing the point of the hammer within the body. The trigger-nose catches under the hammer-catch, and prevents any further movement of the hammer.

(*b*) *Continuous action.*—On pulling the trigger, the trigger-nose engages the hammer catch and revolves the hammer. The action is the same then as when cocking by hand, except that instead of the trigger-nose engaging the bent in the toe of the hammer, the hammer is revolved until the trigger-nose trips clear of the hammer-catch, when the hammer is released and fires the cartridge.

Safety arrangement.

When the trigger has been released, the hammer-catch is bearing on the heel of the trigger, so the hammer cannot move further forward and reach the cartridge until the trigger is again pressed and the catch has tripped clear of the trigger-nose.

Instructions for Cleaning, and Clearing Jammed Pull-through or Flannelette from, Barrels of ·303-inch Rifles and Carbines by Armourers.

(Instructions for cleaning by the soldier are given in the Musketry Regulations.)

(1) *N.B.*—The oil used must be "oil, petroleum, Russian, lubricating." No other lubricant is to be used for the bore of barrels, except that and paraffin mixed when cleaning with brass wire and jute and emery, as detailed below.

(2) *To clean a rusty barrel with the double pull-through.*—All barrels which are slightly rusty inside will be thoroughly cleaned by the armourer. A double pull-through, having a hand loop at one end to enable it to be used with assistance, is supplied for this purpose. It will be used without flannelette (the gauze being expanded as described hereunder) in the following manner :—

Remove the bolt; well oil the gauze of the pull-through, drop the weight through the barrel from the breech, clamp the muzzle guide on the muzzle of the barrel to prevent damage by friction of the cord, and pull the gauze to and fro until the rust is removed; care being taken to draw the pull-through out of the barrel in line with the bore, as any friction of the pull-through cord with the sides of the chamber at the breech causes the chamber to become oval, and thus renders the barrel unserviceable. When the gauze of the pull-through, in consequence of frequent use, ceases to fit the barrel tightly, narrow strips of flannelette or paper may be inserted under each side to increase its diameter.

(3) *To clean rusty barrels with brass wire emery, and jute.*—The eye of the rods Nos. 2, 3, or 4 for wire will be filled with from 50 to 60 strands of brass wire, No. 26 S.W.G., hard, cut in 3-inch lengths, the ends will be pressed back along the length of the rod. The wire, being well oiled with a mixture of two volumes of "oil, petroleum, Russian, lubricating," to one volume of paraffin oil, will be inserted in the muzzle end of the barrel, the arm being held in a vice; the muzzle guide* will then be clamped on the muzzle and the rod worked up and down the bore to remove the rust.

In the case of magazine carbines and short rifles the nose cap will have to be removed before using the muzzle guide.

If a barrel is very rusty it will be found easier to remove the rust if the muzzle of the barrel is plugged, and oil poured in from the breech end, and left to soak for a few hours.

After loosening the rust, wipe out the barrel with the rod,

---

* When a muzzle guide becomes worn in the cleaning rod guide hole, particular notice should be taken that there is no friction between the cleaning rod and the bore of the barrel, which is liable to render the barrel unserviceable.

cleaning No. 1, for jute, and examine (the jute for this rod will be cut in about 8-inch lengths).

If a barrel is found to require further cleaning, coil the jute round so that it fits the bore tightly, and sprinkle on a little flour emery, replace in the barrel, and after clamping on the muzzle guide work the rod well up and down until the barrel is clean.

The rust being removed, a slightly pitted surface will usually remain, this should be greased with " oil, petroleum, Russian, lubricating."

To preserve the wire when the rods are not in use a cartridge case cut short at the shoulder will be found useful as a cap.

Rods, cleaning, for wire, are supplied in three lengths, No. 2 for long rifles, No. 3 for carbines, and No. 4 for short rifles, arranged so that the wire cannot pass beyond the front end of the chamber, owing to the difficulty of withdrawing it if it does so.

Rod, cleaning, No. 2, if fitted with the " Bush, stop, rod. cleaning, No. 2," is suitable for short rifles.

The rod, cleaning, No. 1 for jute is made of one length suitable for rifles (long and short) and carbines.

(4) *To clear the barrel when pull-through becomes broken and jammed.*—Screw the "plug clearing plain" on the "rod tool clearing ·303-inch arms," and place it in the barrel at the end nearest the jammed flannelette; compress the flannelette and cord as much as possible, then withdraw the rod and plug, unscrew the plug and screw on the bit spoon, pass this into the barrel and turn, pressing firmly against the jammed material; the spoon bit should be withdrawn after about six turns, and the bit, screw, inserted to withdraw the *cut* material. Very much pressure should not be applied to the bit spoon; neither should it be turned too many times before withdrawing, as it only chokes when the spoon is filled; care also should be taken that all the material cut by the spoon bit is withdrawn by the bit screw before again using the spoon bit; this should be continued until the bit screw will withdraw the remaining cord and gauze.

NOTE.—No rod of soft metal or wood is ever to be used by armourers in cleaning or clearing the bore of barrels of ·303-inch arms, only the rods issued which are of hard steel should be used.

Clearing the Envelope of a Bullet or a Cartridge Case.

Should the envelope of a bullet be left in the lead, or the base of the cartridge case separate circumferentially, the "plug, clearing, split," is used. Insert the plug with the cut-away portion of the rim on the left side of the chamber, close the bolt, and in opening the breech the extractor will draw the plug out of the chamber and the nibs on the split end of the plug, engaging with the envelope or the case, will draw it also out of the chamber.

Should this fail to act in clearing the envelope, the "plug, clearing, plain," attached to the rod and passed down from the muzzle will remove the obstruction.

MAXIM GUNS IN THE SERVICE.

Gun, Maxim, ˙45-in.—Martin-Henry Chamber.
Introduced into L.S. January, 1891.

Gun, Maxim, ˙303-in.—Magazine Rifle Chamber.
Introduced into L.S. July, 1893.

Gun, Maxim, ˙303-in. Converted Mk. I.—February, 1899.
(Converted from ˙45-in. Maxim guns.)

Gun, Maxim, ˙303-in. Converted Mk. II.—February, 1902.

The ˙45-in. gun will only be met with in the Colonies and Egypt.

The average weight for all = 60 lbs.
The normal rate of fire = 450 rds. per min.
Water in barrel casing boils at 600 rds. with rapid fire.
  „   „   „   evaporates 1½ pints for each 1000 rds. if firing continuous.
˙45-in. Sighted up to about 2000 yds.
˙303-in. Converted „ 2500 „
˙303-in. Guns   „ 2900 „

The conversion of ˙45-in. guns to ˙303-in. converted Mark I consists in the substitution of ˙303-in. barrels, and the altering of various components to suit the smaller calibre barrel. The latter is of the same external diameter as the ˙45-in. barrel, and has a special ball attachment.

The converted Mark II gun differs from last in being fitted with the Service ˙303-in. barrel and attachment for ball firing.

With these guns the ball detachment must always be used for firing owing to the heavier components. The fusee spring for Mark I should be 10 to 12 lbs., and with the Mark II same as for the Service gun, viz., 5 to 7 lbs.

The action, stripping, &c., is identical, for all practical purposes, to that of the Service ˙303-in. gun.

·303-in. MAXIM MACHINE GUN.

Nomenclature of Parts of Gun.

Barrel .: ..	With asbestos packing; gunmetal valve.
Barrel Casing..	With ejector tube spring; steam tube with slide valve; keeper screw; packing gland; asbestos packing; two screwed plugs, each with chain, S hooks, and stud; cork plug with chain and S hooks.
Breech Casing	With buffer spring; check lever with collar and split pin; slides, right and left; trigger bar; fusee spring box.
Cover	With joint pin, collar, and fixing pin; cover lock, with piston, spring, and stop screw; ammunition label with four rivets; cover springs.
Crank	With crank pin and fixing pin; connecting rod; adjustable with cotter and fixing pin; crank handle and fixing pin; fusee with chain, spring, and adjusting screw.
Feed Block ..	With slide; top and bottom levers with spring fixing pin; top and bottom pawls, with axis pin; slide springs; feed block spring; band roller with axis pin, collar, and fixing pin.
Lock	Consisting of casing with side levers and screwed head; extractor levers, right and left; extractor with spring and fixing pin; gib with gib spring and cover; extractor stop with keeper and fixing pins; sear with spring and axis pin; trigger with axis and fixing pins; tumbler with axis and fixing pins; firing pin Mk. I;* lock spring, with axis and fixing pins; keeper bracket.
Rear Cross-piece	With fixing pin; firing lever with spring and axis pin; safety catch and axis pin; piston and spring; shutter with pivot screw; milled heads with leather washers, and oil brushes.
Side Plates ...	Side plate, right, with side plate spring; side plate, left, with connecting rod spring.
Sight, Fore ..	With fixing screw.
Sight, Tangent	Consisting of stem, graduated plate, and two fixing screws; slide with pinion, pawl, and fixing pin; tangent sight slide spring; milled head and fixing screw; axis pin; tangent sight spring and piston.

---

* A Mark II pattern firing pin has been introduced to govern future manufacture, provided with a removable striker, which is held in position by a fixing pin.

Tools used for stripping, cleaning, &c., carried in the spare part box,* are as follows :—

Designation of Tool.	No.	Use of Tool.
Plugs, clearing ...	1	For removal of separated cartridge cases from the chamber.
Keys, gib ...	1	For screwing up or removal of G.M. valve.
Hammers ...	1	Various uses.
Punches, No. 1 ...	1	For riveting tumbler axis pins in old pattern locks.
„ „ 2 ...	1	For driving out large axis pins and starting smaller pins.
„ „ 3 ...	1	For driving out sear axis and smaller pins.
„ „ 4, Mk. II ...	1	For extractor spring fixing pins and to act as a pilot pin for lock spring axis.
Pliers, cutting, pairs	1	For " wiring " axis pins and various uses.
Wrenches, pin ...	1	For removal or replacement of packing gland.
Spanners, shifting ...	1	Various uses.
Screwdrivers, large	1	Do.
„ small	1	Do.
„ bent ...	1	Do.
Balances, spring	1	Weighing various springs.
Mallets, raw hide, No. 5 ...	1	For removal or replacement of rear cross-piece and breech casing.

In addition to the above, 1 clearing rod, brass water vessel, funnel, tool for repairing belts, pull-through double, 2 wire gauzes, and a water bag are also provided.

* Except the mallet, which is with the armourer's tools.

STRIPPING '303-in. MAXIM.

The gun is stripped in the following order :—

Note.—All pins are driven in from R—L, and out *vice versa.*

(1) *Lock and Feed Block :*—Raise cover, turn crank handle on to buffer spring, see that extractor drops, place finger between extractor and stop, raise lock and allow crank handle to come slowly back on to check lever; slide live cartridges out of extractor. Give lock ⅛ turn to the left and lift off. Lift feed block out by pulling it upwards.

(2) *Fuzee Spring Box :*—With right hand at the rear and left at front, press box forward until clear of lugs and remove. Disconnect fuzee chain and remove box and spring. Care should be taken to throw no cross strain on the chain.

(3) *Tangent Sight and Cover Lock :*—Drive out axis pin of stem and remove with its piston and spring. Press in cover lock and with small screwdriver remove stop screw; the lock with its piston and spring can be removed.

(4) *Cover :*—Drive out fixing pin of cover joint pin, remove collar and joint pin, and take off cover.

(5) *Rear Cross-piece :*—Drive out tapered fixing pin, grasp with the left hand the left handle of the rear cross-piece, slightly raise the casing and with mallet strike top edges of casing alternately until rear cross-piece is clear of the dovetails on the casing.

(6) *Slides (R. and L.) and Check Lever :*—Pull out the slides. Drive out split pin from check lever, remove collar and check lever.

(7) *Recoiling Portion :*—Fold back connecting rod on to crank, turn crank handle vertical and draw out to the rear the recoiling portion. Disconnect side plates by dropping and springing out to one side. If necessary the crank handle can be driven off with a drift and hammer, and the fuzee unscrewed from left bearing of crank, but as a rule these parts are not required to be stripped.

(8) *Foresight :*—Remove fixing screw and foresight.

(9) *Breech and Barrel Casing :*—Rest barrel casing on a table or bench, filling hole uppermost and breech casing clear of bench, place left hand under breech casing and strike the top edges alternately with a mallet and the casings will come apart.

Note.—Care must be taken not to strike the barrel casing, and the blows should be struck as close to the dovetailing as possible.

(10) *Steam Tube Packing Gland and Ejector Tube Spring :*—Up-end the barrel casing so that packing gland is uppermost,

remove keeper screw and unscrew the steam tube. Unscrew and remove the packing gland and packing. Lift ejector tube spring with point of screwdriver and tap out the spring with drift and hammer.

(11) *Lock.*—(1) Release lock spring and lay the lock on bench left side uppermost. Then drive out sear, tumbler, and lock spring axis pins. (2) Remove keeper bracket, lock spring, tumbler, firing pin, extractor levers, and sear. (3) Drive out trigger axis pin, extractor stop keeper pin, remove trigger, extractor stop, and slide extractor from face of lock casing. (4) Push out gib spring cover, take out gib spring and gib. (5) Drive out extractor spring fixing pin, and remove extractor spring.

(12) *Feed Block.*—(1) Drive out spring fixing pin of top and bottom levers, drive out bottom lever and remove top lever and slide. (2) Drive out axis pin of bottom pawls and remove pawls with feed block spring. (3) Drive out fixing pin of band roller axis pin, remove collar, axis pin and band roller. (4) Remove top pawls from slide by pressing them outwards. The springs for pawls if weak or broken are only to be removed by an armourer or qualified artificer.

(13) *Tangent Sight.*—(1) Remove the top fixing screw of graduated plate. (2) Run the slide off the stem. (3) Remove fixing screw of the milled head, and lift the latter off the slide. (4) Remove fixing pin, pawl, and pinion from slide. (5) Remove bottom fixing screw of graduated plate and remove latter from the stem. (6) Place the milled head, face upwards, on a bench, then with a drift applied to the rectangular nib on " spring slide " knock the latter down flush with the face when it can be lifted out with the pliers.

(14) *Rear Cross-piece.*—(1) Drive out axis pin of firing lever, and remove the latter with its spiral spring. (2) Drive out axis pin of safety catch, and lift out the latter, also the piston and spring from their seating. (3) Remove pivot screw and shutter. (4) Unscrew, from the handles, the milled heads with their leather washers, and oil brushes.

REPLACEMENT OF DEFECTIVE PARTS OF THE LOCK.

Should any of the components belonging to the lock become defective, they can be replaced, from the spare parts, without stripping the lock right down. Proceed as follows :—

(1) *Sear.*—Fully cock, lift the sear, and *hang up* the firing pin with the tumbler and trigger ; with the lock on a bench, left side up, drive out the sear axis pin, and remove the sear with its spring.

(2) *Tumbler.*—Fully cock, thus hanging up the firing pin on the sear ; drive out the axis pin of tumbler, *pull the trigger slightly*, and lift out tumbler.

Note.—Care should be taken not to allow the screwed head to lift the sear once the tumbler has been removed.

(3) *Trigger.*—Fire the lock, drive out the lock spring axis pin, remove keeper bracket, extractor levers, and lock spring ; next drive out the trigger axis pin and remove the trigger.

(4) *Firing Pin.*—Proceed as for (3) but do not remove the trigger. Remove the tumbler axis pin and tumbler, raise the sear, push the screwed head out of its way and the firing pin will drop out.

(5) *Gib, gib spring, or extractor spring.*—This will necessitate the removal of the extractor from the face of lock casing. Fire the lock, drive out lock spring axis pin, remove keeper bracket and extractor levers ; next drive out keeper pin of extractor stop, remove latter and slide the extractor off the lock casing ; push out gib spring cover, and remove the spring or gib, as the case may be. If extractor spring requires replacing drive out its fixing pin and remove.

Note.—The serviceable components are replaced in the reverse order.

ASSEMBLING '303-in. MAXIM GUN.

Reverse all the foregoing operations, with the exception that recoiling portions must be replaced before the packing and packing gland. The barrel and breech casing will have to be turned upside down, *i.e.*, filling hole down, and bottom plate of breech casing uppermost; care must be taken that the "ejector tube spring" is in position before joining the casings together.

When assembling "feed block," the longer of the two bottom pawls should always be placed at the front.

When assembling the tangent sight it will be found convenient to place the slide on the stem before attaching the milled head; in this position the pinion is prevented from turning with the pawl when engaging the arms of the spring slide outside the lugs on the pawl.

When assembled, lubricate the recoiling portions,* and weigh all springs. Ejector tube spring must be weighed before joining breech and barrel casing.

Weight of springs.—The various springs, when tested or weighed, should be within the following limits :—

				Remarks.
Lock Spring ...	from 12 to 14 lbs.	{	When the lock is fully cocked.
Gib „ ...	„ 4 „ 6 „	) When pressed down flush with the	
Extractor „ ...	„ 4 „ 6 „	) face of extractor.	
Fuzee „ ...	„ 5 „ 7 „		
Fuzee Spring when Ball Attachment is used	from 8 to 10 lbs.		
Ejector Tube Spring „	2½ „ 4 „		

To move recoiling portion, lock in position and fully cocked ; not more than 4 lbs.

To test the latter, remove fuzee spring, see that lock is cocked, turn crank handle vertical and grasp it with right hand, and the fuzee with the left, and work recoiling parts backwards and forwards a few times. Now push recoiling parts right forward and apply ring of balance over knob on crank handle and pull toward the rear, slightly above the horizontal ; the pull should not exceed 4 lbs., if it does reduce the quantity of packing either at gland in front or in cannelure at rear, as may appear desirable.

---

* The recoiling portions should be worked backwards and forwards to ease the packing, distribute the lubricant, &c., so that the friction is no more than 4 lbs.

D

To examine the lock without using gauges.—Remove from the gun, hold it in the left hand, with the extractor at its highest ; test the bents of firing pin and sear by fully cocking, raising the sear slowly and noting that it does not release the firing pin too soon* ; if it does, it indicates rounded or shallow bents. Next, note that the tumbler and trigger bents hold the firing pin when sear is released. Next cock the lock and fire from both sear and trigger; examine point of firing pin and see that it is not damaged or flattened. Compress the lock spring, see that the extractor or extractor levers work freely; it should fall by its own weight, and should be at the highest point when reversed so that the trigger is uppermost and the screwed head is about to release the sear.

Examine the cartridge grooves of extractor and see that there are no burrs or other damage. Weigh the lock, gib, and extractor springs. Replace the lock in the gun and see that the extractor rises to its correct height, *i.e.*, high enough for the horns to clear the solid cams.

Now ascertain that the lock is properly supported in the firing position by the connecting rod, *i.e.*, connecting rod is neither *too long* nor *too short*—if the former, a jam will occur as the extractor cannot rise ; if the latter, a premature opening of breach and partial separation of cartridge case will result.

Proceed as follows :—

Open the cover, turn crank handle on to buffer, raise lock and insert in the extractor the special dummy cartridge supplied for armourers (*vide* para. 6489, List of Changes), lower the lock and allow it to go slowly forward to the closed position ; if it goes home easily and the crank handle reaches the check lever without any pressure of the hand, it shows that the connecting rod is *too short* ; the lock should be raised, cotter pin removed, and a washer and cotter pin of suitable thickness substituted. When correctly adjusted it should require a gentle pressure of the hand to send the lock home and the crank handle on to the check lever.

Note.—A cotter pin and washer bearing the same number should be used, and the thinnest should be tried first ; it may be necessary to use more than one washer, when the cotter pin of the smallest washer should be used.

---

* The outer or tail end of sear should move an appreciable distance before the firing pin is free.

ACTION OF THE MECHANISM.

The gun is prepared for auto-fire by hand, as follows :—

1st motion of crank handle.—On revolving the crank handle on to the buffer spring the lock is drawn to the rear, the extractor horns riding along the "solid cams" until they reach the ends of cams, when the extractor drops, partly by its own weight and assisted by the cover springs. The revolving of the crank adds to the *initial tension* of fuzee spring by the chain being wound round the fuzee, and on releasing the crank handle the fuzee spring causes the lock to fly forward, and the extractor, acted upon by the side and extractor levers, rises and seizes the cartridge which has been brought up into position by pulling the belt through the feed block from right to left with the left hand.

2nd motion of crank handle.—On again revolving the crank handle to the front the lock is drawn to the rear, taking with it the live cartridge from belt, the extractor drops, thus bringing the cartridge in line with the chamber, and on the lock going forward the second time this cartridge is placed in the chamber and the extractor rises to engage a second cartridge, which has been drawn into position in feed block as before detailed.

During the passage of lock to the rear the screwed head on side levers (due to the reciprocating motion of crank) presses down the tail end of tumbler, revolving it on its axis pin, and causing its head, which is engaged with firing pin, to draw back the latter until its bent is engaged by the bent on sear, thus cocking the lock and compressing the lock spring between the firing pin and trigger. On going forward the screwed head and connecting rod tend to straighten themselves, and the former lifts the sear, leaving the firing pin held by the tumbler bent engaging with that of the trigger. The gun is now ready for *rapid fire.*

To fire.—On lifting the safety catch and pressing the firing lever the trigger bar is drawn to the rear; the bar engaging with the tail of trigger pulls it also to the rear, thus releasing the tumbler and firing pin; the latter acted upon by the lock spring flies forward, striking the cap of cartridge and firing the gun.

Immediately on firing, the pressure of gas causes the barrel and side plates to recoil for about 1 inch, and the arm on crank handle coming into contact with the resistance piece forces the curved face on crank handle to *roll* on the resistance piece and itself, thus imparting a rotary or downward motion to the crank; this motion causes the lock to be drawn back and the crank handle to strike the buffer spring. At the same time as this motion is being imparted to the crank the fuzee winds the chain around it, thus further extending the fuzee spring. As the lock moves to the rear it takes the empty case from chamber and live cartridge from belt, the extractor drops, thus bringing empty case in line with ejector tube, and live cartridge in line with chamber. The recoil of barrel and side plates imparts a lateral motion through the top and bottom levers to the feed block slide, and the pawls on slide engage a cartridge in the belt ready to bring it up into position in feed block. When the energy of recoil is absorbed the fuzee spring asserts itself and carries side plates and barrel back into firing position, feeding up the cartridge, the spring unwinds the chain from fuzee revolving the crank and forcing the lock to its normal position, the extractor places empty case in ejector tube and live round in chamber, then rises and seizes the cartridge in feed block.

At the instant the extractor reaches the firing position the screwed head releases the sear and firing pin, the motions being continued so long as firing lever is kept pressed and trigger bar held back, until the ammunition in belt is expended.

Note.—To fire single shots only, revolve crank handle, pull belt through, and let go handle. This places live cartridge in extractor. Revolve crank a second time, *do not touch belt*, this places live cartridge in line with chamber, and on letting go crank handle the lock places it in chamber; extractor rises, but *does not engage another cartridge in feed block*. On firing, a fresh cartridge is fed up, and it will be only necessary to turn crank handle on to buffer spring to repeat the single shots.

Single shots can also be fired with the gun prepared for auto-fire by pressing the firing lever quickly, groups of four or five shots may also be fired, but this requires considerable practice.

STOPPAGES OR JAMS.

May be classed under two headings :—

I. *Temporary.*—Which are usually due to—

    (*a*) Failure of some part of the mechanism, which is generally duplicated, and therefore easily replaced, or it may be defective ammunition.

    (*b*) Want of knowledge of the working parts of the mechanism, or neglect in preparing for action.

II. *Prolonged.*—Due to breakages or defects in the mechanism, which require time and skilled assistance to put right, the gun being put out of action for a considerable period.

The cause of a stoppage or jam in the action of the gun during firing can, as a rule, be quickly detected by noting the position of crank handle, the position taken up by the latter showing the exact place where the lock has been arrested in its backward or forward movement.

Whenever a stoppage occurs, first see if barrel is home by ascertaining whether there is any space between the front edges of the crank bearings and breech casing, if the barrel is not home it will be due to either the "g.m. valve" working loose or a "fault in feed." The latter can be quickly ascertained, without opening cover, by feeling if the feed block slide is "fast" or "loose"—if the former a fault in feed is indicated, if the latter it is probably the valve that is at fault.

The above has reference to the more common "jams" that occur. There are, however, a number of incidental stoppages that the position of crank handle does not make clear ; these are enumerated further on.

When a *Temporary* stoppage necessitates the replacement of a lock, feed block, or other spare component, the part removed should be repaired as soon as possible so as to make it again available for use.

Position of Crank Handle

There are four positions (approximately) which the crank handle occupies when a " jam " occurs :—

1st Position.—At or near the vertical. (Barrel Home.)

This shows that the lock has recoiled the length of a live round, and the " extractor horns" may be above or below the ends of solid cams.

Probable cause.—(1) Heavy fuzee spring. (2) Deteriorated ammunition. (3) Excessive friction due to want of oil, etc. (4) Weak or broken gib spring.

Explanation.—The energy of recoil is expended in trying to *tension* the fuzee spring, the latter being overloaded, or, assuming that the weight of fuzee spring is correct, by a considerable portion of the energy being absorbed by excessive friction between the working parts, or tight pockets in belt for a similar reason, but in the latter case the barrel will not be quite home.

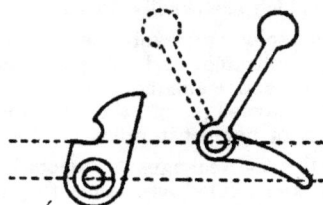

FIRST POSITION

BARREL HOME.

Insufficient pressure due to bad ammunition will also account for a stoppage. When a gib spring breaks the cartridge taken from the feed block by extractor drops in the latter slightly below the mouth of chamber, and therefore cannot enter the latter.

Remedy.—Turn crank handle on to buffer spring, pulley belt to the left and let go, if stoppage repeated proceed as follows:— (1) Lighten fuzee spring, three turns in a contra-clockwise direction. (2) Not likely to be repeated. (3) If spring is at the minimum open cover, lift lock and remove live cartridges, pull belt clear, replace and "hang up" the lock with horns of extractor in rear of solid cams, pull crank handle to the rear and lubricate all bearing surfaces of recoiling parts. Lower lock, pull belt to left, lower cover, and let go the crank handle. (4) Replace lock with spare one from the spare part box. Afterwards replace defective gib or spring.

Note.—If frequent stoppages occur in this position, take the ball attachment into use until a favourable opportunity occurs to investigate more fully.

2nd Position.—At or about 45° from the vertical. (BARREL HOME.)

This shows that the lock has recoiled fully, and is unable to go right forward to the firing position being held back from 1 inch to 2 inches.

Probable cause :—(1) Damaged cartridge. (2) Broken or separated case in chamber. (3) Weak or broken extractor spring. (4) Weak or broken ejector tube spring.

Explanation.—The lock has taken from the feed block a cartridge the exterior shape of which has been altered through some injury, and this cartridge partly enters the chamber and arrests the forward movement of lock according to the position of the injury on the cartridge.

If the lock does not firmly support the cartridge and the breech opens prematurely, the case sets back and separates circumferentially either at the neck or close to the base. thus leaving a portion in the chamber which prevent the insertion of another round.

SECOND POSITION.

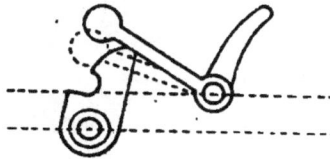

BARREL HOME.

Note.—With frequent separations the connecting rod should be looked to, and if necessary adjusted as detailed, on page 50.

If the extractor spring breaks the empty case drops below the line of the ejector tube, and thus holds back the lock the length of an empty case, viz., $2\frac{1}{4}$ inches.

Remedy.—Strike crank handle a smart, glancing blow towards the rear with heel of right hand, and if obstruction is cleared carry on, if it remains, proceed as follows:—

(1) Open cover, turn crank handle on to buffer spring, see that extractor drops,* raise lock with left hand; remove the damaged cartridge, lower lock and cover, pull belt through to left, and let go.

(2) Open cover, and turn crank handle on to buffer spring; raise lock as before, examine cartridges in extractor, remove broken case (sometimes it will be found that a portion of a case is adhering to a live cartridge in extractor), remove live cartridge from extractor. Take "clearing plug" with its centre pin fully back, place plug in chamber, lower lock and allow it to go forward until face of extractor is bearing against pin; now press crank handle firmly down, and at the same time with left hand give clearing plug a sharp rocking motion. Now withdraw lock, depress handle of plug, and remove with broken case. Replace live cartridge in extractor, lower lock, pull belt through to left, lower cover, let go crank handle, and proceed as before.

(3) Change lock with spare one, &c. The empty case will be resting on the projecting nib of spring instead of above it.

(4) Exchange the spring for spare one. It will be necessary to take breech and barrel casing apart. This jam may occur when firing at fairly high targets or big angles of elevation, the defective spring allowing empties to fall back into breech casing.

---

* On no account must the extractor be allowed to rise while it contains live cartridges, as with the cover open there would be danger of accident.

3rd Position.—At or about 15°—20° from horizontal (BARREL HOME, or nearly home).

THIRD POSITION.

BARREL HOME.
(OR NOT HOME.)

If " barrel home," this shows that the lock is almost home, but the extractor is unable to rise to the firing position.

If " barrel not home," and feed block slide jammed, a fault in feed is indicated.

Probable cause.—(1) Thick rimmed cartridge. (2) Damaged cartridge grooves in extractor. (3) Light fuzee spring. (4) Want or oil, of excessive friction during the final movement of lock.

Explanation.—If the rim of a cartridge or the grooves in the extractor should be damaged, the extractor in rising will meet with a considerable resistance, and as this is the moment the fuzee spring is at its weakest, the extractor is unable to rise to the firing position and grip the cartridge in feed block.

A light fuzee spring would give a similar result. Excessive friction would absorb the energy necessary to raise the extractor.

A *badly filled belt* with loose pockets, *damaged strips*, or a *belt box* at an undue angle to the feed block would also absorb a large portion of the necessary energy and cause a stoppage, but in these latter cases the barrel would not go home.

Remedy.—Strike crank handle as for 2nd position, and it will probably clear the obstruction ; if not, proceed as follows :—(1) Open cover, push extractor down, at same time turn crank handle on to buffer and raise lock, remove defective cartridge, which will usually be found in feed block. Lower lock and cover, pull belt, &c., and let go crank handle. (2) Strike crank handle as before, if it fails to go home, replace lock by spare one. If certain that it is not the ammunition (cartridge rims) that is at fault, run the thumb nail along the knife edges of extractor grooves and the position of burrs, &c., can be located. An armourer or artificer should carry out repair. (3) Strike crank handle as before, and if it again jams remove the spring box and increase weight of spring by turning screw in a clockwise direction (6 turns to 1 lb.). (4) Strike handle as before, and if stoppage is repeated open cover, hang up the lock and oil all bearing parts. This is usually

the last thing looked for, as the gun should be well lubricated
before firing takes place.

Note.—Care should be taken to distinguish between "tight
packing" and "want of oil." To discover which fault is present,
weigh the recoiling parts to see if within limits—4 lbs.

4th Position.—Crank handle right down on check lever (BARREL
HOME).

*This position shows that a cartridge has failed to fire, or if it has
fired, as with blank, there has been little or no recoil, the lock remaining in a forward or closed position.*

FOURTH POSITION

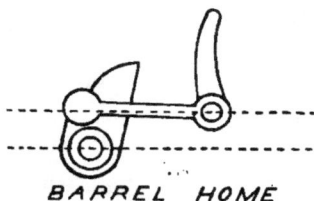

BARREL HOME

Probable cause:—(1) Broken side levers. (2) Broken extractor
levers. (3) Tumbler axis pin worked out. (4) Blank cartridge.
(5) All miss-fires. (6) Broken or flattened point of firing pin.
(7) Broken lock spring.

Explanation.—As the causes given are mostly mechanical
defects in the mechanism the results briefly explained are as
follows :—

(1) and (2).—The extractor will not rise, but the lock will be
cocked, and on pressing the firing lever will be fired, giving an
audible indication that the spring and bents are correct.

(3). The crank handle can only be moved a short distance owing
to the pin fouling the side levers.

(4) and (5).—Insufficient or no recoil to work the parts is cleared
by turning crank handle on to buffer spring and pulling the belt,
if a miss-fire the defective round should be looked for amongst
the empties.

(6) and (7) call for no remark ; insufficient blow on cap to ignite
the composition.

Remedy.—(1) and (2) Open the cover and it will be seen that
extractor has not risen. Only one remedy, replace the lock by
spare one, &c.

(3) Practically puts gun out of action, and in order to clear it
the recoiling portion will have to be removed. Remove feed
block, check lever, rear cross-piece, slides, (R and L), and crank
handle ; the latter will have to be driven off far enough to clear

58

the resistance piece. Pull recoiling portions to the rear, at the same time breech casing must be sprung open and push in tumbler axis pin, carefully remove the lock, reassemble various parts, including spare lock, and carry on.

(4) Turn crank handle on to buffer spring, pull belt, and let go.

(5) As for last; by this action, defective cartridge is placed in ejector tube and fresh one in chamber.

(6) If after trying a second cartridge it still fails, open cover, remove cartridges from lock, and see if cap has been struck; if not, or if struck very slightly, examine firing pin to see if it is either broken or flattened. If either of the latter, replace by spare lock, &c.

(7) Try again as for the last, open cover, and if extractor is at its highest it indicates a broken lock spring or firing pin. Replace lock by spare one, &c.

FAULTS IN FEED.

In nearly all cases the barrel will not be able to go right home, therefore the *crank bearings* will be *showing a space in front*, and *feed block slide* will be *stuck fast.*

Probable cause.—(1) Long cartridge (will not pass on to the cartridge and bullet stops). (2) Damaged cartridge (same as for last). (3) Badly filled belt. (4) Top pawls catching strips after last round has been fed up to ready position.

Jams also occur through the long strips getting bent, or cartridges jarring loose during firing, especially with an old or worn belt. If the belt box is at an undue angle a jam outside feed block will be the result.

Explanation.—The effect of a fault in feed is that the top pawls having engaged behind a cartridge in the belt are unable, owing to some obstruction, to carry the cartridge up to the bullet and cartridge stops in the feed block. The slide which carries these pawls is connected to the barrel, and the result is the latter is prevented from going home. The distance it is held back will depend on the position of the slide in block, so that the 3rd position of crank handle will not always be the position in which a fault in the feeding action occurs.

Remedy.—The quickest way to clear the above jams would be to remove the feed block and belt complete, and take the spare feed block and fresh belt into use.

The *jammed block and belt* meanwhile *being put right, ready for replacement* when a favourable opportunity occurs.

MISS-FIRES.

Miss-fires are usually caused through some of the following:—
(1) Worn point of firing pin. (2) Weak lock spring. (3) Side levers worn. (4) Extractor levers worn. (5) Bent on firing pin

or sear worn (or shallow). (6) Defective or deteriorated
ammunition.

In addition to the foregoing stoppages a varied number of
other causes are given below in detail. They are not of a common
occurrence, but have been known to happen, and are included
here to enable a detachment to recognize them and apply such
rumedy as may be advisable.

OTHER STOPPAGES.

A { *At Rapid fire.*—1st Position of crank handle and *Barrel
Home.* (1)* Tight pockets in belt. (2) Barrel worn in
lead of chamber. (3) Broken gib. (4) Broken cover
springs. (5) Broken firing pin at tumbler way, or recess
for lock spring. (6) Broken head or tail of tumbler.

B { 3rd Position of crank handle with *Barrel Home.* (1)
Heavy gib or extractor spring. (2) Strained firing pin or
tumbler. (3) Slightly damaged cartridge. (4) Dirty or
rusty chamber. (5) Tight packing. (6) Bad feed. (7),
Side plates damaged or bent. (8) Buckled extractor
spring. (9) Fouling or erosion in ball attachment. (10)
Firing pin hole in extractor burred. (11) Screwed head
of lock not home. (12)* Gunmetal valve worked loose.
(13) Mark II connecting rod too long.

C { 4th Position of crank handle, with *Barrel Home.* (1) Broken
feed arm of side plate. (2) Broken stud on feed block
slide. (3) Broken top or bottom lever of feed block. (4)
Broken trigger bar at knuckle joint. (5) Shutter pivot
screw worked loose or unscrewed.

D { AT SINGLE FIRE. 4th Position of crank handle. *Barrel not
home.* (1) Heavy fuzee spring. (2) Light charge. (3)
Want of oil. (4) Broken head or tail of tumbler. (5)
Broken firing pin. (6) Barrel worn.

With regard to the above stoppages, briefly explained:—
" A."—Denotes that the lock has recoiled, at least the full length
of a cartridge, but the extractor has not dropped, or if it has,
the bullet is not in line with the chamber. " B."—Denotes the
inability of the extractor to rise after the lock has gone right
forward. " C."—That the breech is properly closed; this can be
readily distinguished from a " miss-fire " by the fact that it is
possible to load by hand, and in case of 1, 2, and 3 to fire the
gun without getting any " feed," and in the case of 4 and 5 not
to hear the lock fire when the firing lever is pressed. " D."—
The faults given are all liable to be brought about by loading
the gun for *single fire*, but if the gun is set for *rapid fire* and
single shots are fired deliberately by tapping the firing lever
these faults would not occur; with 4 and 5 the " tumbler " and
" firing pin " are damaged at the moment of firing. It should be
noted that it is *single fire*, and the *barrel is not home.*

---

* With these two jambs the barrel will not go home.

CONDEMNATION OF MAXIM ·303-INCH GUN BARRELS.

As far as the *Land Service* is concerned, Maxim machine-gun barrels will, in future, be condemned as unserviceable if they fail to reach the standard of accuracy detailed in Equipment Regulations (see para. 179, E.R., Part I, 1909, Section VI), condemnation by gauging being abolished.

The sentencing of unserviceable barrels D.P. will be done by the Chief Inspector of Small Arms, Enfield Lock, as hitherto.

For *Naval Service* the following is the procedure for condemnation of barrels :—

(1) Barrel cleaned and free from metallic fouling, etc., as with rifles and carbines. The ·303-in. plug should run.

(2) The coppering on exterior at muzzle and breech end not to be chipped or blistered.

(3) The ·307-in. plug enters $\frac{1}{4}$ inch at muzzle.

(4). The ·309-in. ,,   ,,   1 inch at breech.

(*i.e.*, to line engraved on rods, plug.)

(5) The No. 1 lead plug enters the breech $\frac{7}{16}$ inch.